the
BLENDER
GIRL

the
BLENDER
GIRL

super-easy, super-healthy
MEALS, SNACKS, DESSERTS & DRINKS

tess masters

photography by anson smart

TEN SPEED PRESS
Berkeley

contents

birth of the blender girl

Hello, my name is Tess, and I'm a *blendaholic*.

And when it comes to passing on my addiction to others, I'm also an enabler. But fear not. This habit (one you may soon find yourself hooked on, too) is healthy, and comes with a blender-load of positive side effects.

We can't bottle time, so in our hectic lives we've taken to bottling, canning, boxing, and vacu-packing everything else. Convenience foods offer a quick (and often, virtually empty) way to fill up on the fly, and it's only human that we make the trade-off.

But we don't *have* to compromise on health, nutrition, or good eating just because we've got pressing things to do. Enter the blender, which makes healthy fast food possible. This phenomenal machine is the greatest culinary gift bestowed on us since fire and spoons! Blending makes life easier, levels the playing field in the kitchen, and allows anybody to whip up nutrient-dense, tasty foods with limited skills and time.

No, we don't check our teeth at the door. While this book *does* contain a repertoire of drinks, smoothies, and soups, you'll find more here than food to sip, glug, or scoop up in a spoon. My recipes are blender centered but by no means blender only. I favor blender-inspired dishes—appetizers, snacks, salads, desserts, and easy main dishes you can attack with your trusty knife and fork. The blended components—sauces, spreads, and condiments—play a vital role in these dishes; a delicious pesto or homemade mayo can elevate that basic bowl of pasta or plate of steamed vegetables from bland and boring to brilliant.

So, okay, yes, in addition to being an addict and an enabler, I'm also a zealot! But I hasten to say, not an evangelist. I'm neither a foodie nor a chef nor a gourmet shopaholic. I'm a regular person and a self-taught cook who just loves food.

i became the blender girl by accident

I felt constantly lethargic in my teens, and was eventually diagnosed with Epstein-Barr. At the suggestion of a naturopath, I gave up gluten, dairy, and meat, and felt better almost overnight. I'd been brought up on a conventional meat-and-three-veg diet, and was, indeed, both gluten and dairy intolerant. This was my awakening to food as medicine and a revolution in the way I ate. I was now an omnivore with a dilemma, but would have to wait years to read Michael Pollan's eye-opening book. I pursued a keen interest in the relationship between food and health, studied nutrition science, and took cooking classes to develop my culinary skills.

In my early twenties, my friend Toni introduced me to macrobiotics, which became an important part of my ongoing journey of discovery. However, after following this regime religiously, I still didn't feel as good as I knew I could.

Frustrated that I hadn't found the golden ticket, I was convinced that there had to be, somewhere out there, a perfect whole-foods diet that would be my magical "cure." As a perfectionist, I was going to master the art of my own health even if it killed me!

In my self-imposed and largely self-directed crusade, I tried countless whole-foods diets. I became vegetarian, then vegan, discovered the benefits of raw foods, practiced Body Ecology anti-candida principles, employed Chinese yin and yang strategies, dabbled in Ayurvedic techniques, tried out the blood-type theory, embraced the pH Miracle alkalinity plan, and whipped up zillions of green smoothies. Yes, I really *was* one of those people who finds the answer every six months. But while all these healthy approaches had things to offer, none was quite one-size-fits-me. When I embraced the concept of bio-individuality—the recognition that no single, blanket health strategy will work for everybody—things shifted.

I supplemented my knowledge with an intuitive-experiential approach, and discovered that flexibility and fluidity, not rigidity, were for me keys to well being. Today I cherry-pick from all of the healthy diets I've tried, working successful practices into my "immune-boosting Tess diet." This diet adapts in response to climate, stress, emotions, physical activity, and specific health questions that arise. I'm a seasonal eater. In the hotter months, I eat a high percentage of raw foods; when it's cold, more cooked foods. But green alkaline smoothies, juices, and soups are year-round staples.

With those as a focus when I started my blog, I got inspiration from my blender, the "s'blended" machine that helps me maintain a healthy lifestyle with ease and great gustatory pleasure. I quickly saw blending not only as a method of food preparation but also as a guiding metaphor for how I live.

the perfect blend

Combining different concepts, flavors, and philosophies plays a crucial part in my ideal balance of food, exercise, work, and fun. While my approach isn't a system exactly, it does add up to a recipe for success and happiness, and one that I believe is worth sharing.

A diet featuring ample quantities and varieties of leafy greens, alkaline vegetables, and raw sprouted nuts, seeds, and grains, combined with daily green juices and smoothies, can be beneficial to just about anyone. In addition to this, each of us will discover that individualized, perfect blend of joyful activities, fulfilling work, loving relationships, time with family, food, exercise, and more. With all this in mind, my recipes aim for versatility and simplicity.

Yes, some of the main dishes require a little time. But often I've structured the involved dishes into movable parts so you can choose how much work you want to put into the final product.

One key word you'll see in my recipes repeatedly is *optional*. A key phrase is *tweak to taste*. Another great advantage of cooking in and around the blender is that, in sharp contrast to most culinary disciplines, such as baking, there is very rarely a point of no return with these recipes. Blend, taste, tweak. And then blend, taste, tweak again. This way, you're not committed until it's just right. Knowing your own tastes and those of the people you're feeding, you'll readily turn that occasional blender bomb into a blender bombshell.

Treat this selection of familiar favorites as a blank canvas for creativity. Whether it's the cream of cauliflower soup (see page 104) that has tasters insisting "there's *gotta* be dairy in this," the sneak-your-veggies-in tomato sauce (see page 203) that turns any pasta or pizza into nutritious family fun food, the potato salad (see page 88) whose blended dressing ensures no spud will be a dud, the apple pie smoothie (see page 62) that's reminiscent of the perfect bite à la mode, the ten-minute chocolate torte (see page 152) that makes chocoholics weak at the knees, or the kale shake (see page 45) that tastes like ice cream and has moved hardened *greenophobes* to beg for more, my recipes are always about health *and* fun. So get plugged in, throw your personality into the mix, and make these blends your own.

find *your* perfect blend

This story is divided into two sections: The Lowdown and The Recipes. If your stomach is growling, plug in your machine, and whirl straight into blending.

Looking to buy a blender, or want to get the most out of your machine? Check out Love Your Blender on page 9. If you're interested in health and nutrition, or in the principles that underlie my recipes, see Healthy Ideas to Blend In (page 15) for the scoop. These nutrition-boosting strategies, which may not immediately register on the palate, *do* have culinary benefits, too; they can lead to better taste and texture with blended food preparation. The section on soaking (see page 21) will on its own help you realize the full nutrient potential of foods, help your blender liquefy them better, and make clear why I say "soak" in many of my recipes.

Enjoy your blending! Life is fast and messy, and things don't have to be perfect. I have the most fun with a rustic, no-frills-and-lots-of-spills, throw-it-all-in approach to fresh foods. After all, we're going to blend it anyway. In fact, *everything* centers around the blender here, and you don't need much else to join in besides a knife, cutting board, and some measuring cups and spoons. There are just a few instances where a food processor or dehydrator is required, or a high-speed blender is essential. I've deliberately used ingredients (in most cases) that are widely available so you don't have to spend your weekly paycheck or supersize your carbon footprint to blend in.

I've shared tips for making killer smoothies (see page 52) and soups (see page 112), and provided a cheat sheet for making most plant-based milks (see page 29). Browse recipes by category and dietary preferences. All of the dishes are gluten-free and vegan—free of dairy, eggs, or other animal products. You can also search the index (see page 214) for recipes that are:

Alkaline: healthy pH power (see page 35).

Nut free: go nuts without peanuts and tree nuts.

Probiotic rich: immune-boosting goodness (see page 30).

Properly combined: use food combining principles (see page 31).

Raw: not cooked and loaded with live enzymes.

Soy free: so good with no soy.

Sugar free: sweet enough without it.

This book is my collection of love letters—to the power of whole foods, to the power of balance, and to everything you can make in the miraculous blender. These loves have helped me find *my* perfect blend on more than one occasion.

Now, on to *your* story. Blend and live!

the lowdown

CHAPTER 1

love your blender

In negotiating with any blender, my tactic is "Let me help you help me!"

Blending is a partnership, a dance (so to speak), between you and your machine. Each make and model has its own moves, complete with virtues and quirks. When you understand your machine's personality, you can work magic together.

I'm a firm believer in matching your blender to *your* personality.

choosing a blender

Shop for a blender like you'd shop for a car. Look at the various brands and ask yourself a few questions: Why am I buying this? What am I going to make in it? When and how often will I use it? Who else will use it? How many people will I be feeding with it?

Review your needs, budget, and available kitchen space, then check out the goods. Read consumer research, and ask friends and family to share their experiences. Give a friend's machine a test drive.

Having tried nearly every machine on the market (yes, I have a pantry full) and considered thousands of opinions from readers, I've decided that with a blender you really *do* get what you pay for. Oster, Sunbeam, KitchenAid, Cuisinart, Breville, Omega, Blendtec, and Vitamix all offer good products, ranging from bare bones to fully loaded, in single-, multi-, and variable-speed models. (For recommendations, see page 12.)

Options can include automatic timers, built-in measuring functions, pre-programmed settings, and heating capabilities. For my money, I'm not interested in all of those bells and whistles. I focus on the power of the motor, the blade construction, and the warranty. I very rarely use pre-programmed settings, opting instead to control my blending manually. Maybe I'm a control freak, but I think one of the virtues of variable speeds is that I can use them to my own preferences, which change with every blend.

Currently the most powerful and versatile blenders are the high-speed models from Omega, Blendtec, and Vitamix, retailing for about $400. Some people see a blender in this price range is an over-the-top purchase. I view it as an investment in a healthy lifestyle, which you can't put a price on. I use my high-speed blender more than I drive my car.

Still, financial commitments and priorities, like culinary habits and aspirations, are individual. If you're only looking to whip up the occasional smoothie, a conventional machine at a basic price point is a good way to go. For us blendaholics, breaking open the piggy bank to go for a top-of-the-line pick is justified.

You *can* prepare my recipes, enjoy great flavors, reap health benefits, and have fun with any machine. The main variable is texture. Soaking ingredients for conventional blenders is critical (see page 21) as they lack the pulverizing and flavor extraction abilities of a high-speed machine when working with nuts, dates, and fibrous foods. Familiarize yourself with your appliance by blending a variety of foods and see how it handles them: hard foods, thick liquids with air bubbles, crushed ice, and so on. You'll also learn which speeds (or speeds in combination) do the best with different foods. These factors help you fine-tune texture within your blender's limits.

care and feeding of your blender

Good blenders are resilient, but not indestructible. Even high-speed varieties need to be treated with respect. This maximizes durability and longevity, and achieves the most effective blends. Some foods you *can* just throw in and blend on high. But with thick consistencies, hard ingredients, or widely varied textures, guiding and assisting the machine can make the difference between blender glitch and blender glory. Whatever your make and model, here are my tips to get the best from it.

soak, don't choke

Soak hard ingredients like nuts, seeds, and dried fruits and vegetables before blending (see page 21). The extra work is worth it to spare your machine undue stress and enhance the texture of your finished dish. Soaked dates blend more easily and soaked sun-dried tomatoes incorporate better and deliver more flavor. The velvety quality of blended soaked cashews, blanched almonds, and macadamias is mind-blowing.

chop, mince, and grate to the best state

Cut up vegetables and mince or grate fibrous foods like beets, carrots, horseradish, and ginger to reduce stress on the motor, layer ingredients in optimal liquefying order, distribute flavors evenly, and achieve the smoothest texture. Food measures more accurately in small pieces and you can add tiny amounts to taste.

liquids, powders, solids, ice

For efficient blending, pour liquids into the container first so the blades move easily when you turn the machine on. Add powdered ingredients—such as cacao, protein mixes, and dried greens—after the liquids and before solids so they don't fly up on ignition and stick to the lid. Next, layer in soft foods like bananas and cucumbers. After that, throw on hard ingredients, such as frozen fruits and raw vegetables. Last to go in is ice, which helps the blades pull all the other ingredients down for even mixing.

---

note: With individual-portion blenders like the Nutribullet, reverse this order. Since you fill, and then invert to blend, put liquids in last.

---

don't overload and it won't explode

Blenders work best when they're not filled to the top. Too much in the container, and the blend's got no room to move. (Too little, and the blades just spin their wheels.) Cramming is a recipe for disaster, particularly with hot liquids. Blending in batches saves time and mess. Scalding has no known health or flavor benefits, and is not sexy.

lock and load

It's tempting to plunk the lid in place and start your engine. But taking time to secure the lid with the force of thunder before letting it rip prevents the Jackson Pollock ceiling fiasco. (Yes, I've done that. The less said the better.)

resist the need, the need for speed

Start on low and work your way up. This reduces wear and tear on the motor, and blends everything better. In making nut milks, a slow start chops the nuts, prepping them to liquefy. Instant blasting sprays food up onto the lid and sides of the carriage, requiring more scraping or leaving chunky bits in your blend.

treat, don't overheat

With extra-thick blends like nut butters, dips, and pastes, process in short intervals (30 to 40 seconds) to prevent overheating and smoking your machine. If you hear your blender struggling (with a high-pitched or grinding noise) or it seems that ingredients are spinning without blending (you've likely got a trapped air bubble), turn off the motor and use a spatula to mix things up. A bit more liquid often makes the difference.

get hot, not burnt

The safest way to blend hot liquids like soups and sauces is to allow them to cool somewhat. Then fill the container halfway, place the lid on firmly, remove the small center lid cap (to let steam escape), and place a dishcloth over the opening. Start on the lowest speed and slowly increase to the highest speed. Removing the center lid cap is not necessary for high-speed blenders, which are designed to handle boiling liquids. Still, it's a good move to place a dishcloth over the lid to avoid burning your hands. Cooling before blending also helps you fine-tune flavors. Extremes of hot and cold dull our taste buds, so you'll get more precise results when you taste-test blends just warm or cool.

clean me, never demean me

Keep your machine sanitary and free of stains by cleaning it right after use. Even a gentle scouring pad can scratch your blender, so don't let food congeal in or on it. To wash your container, rinse out the residual food as soon as you've poured out your blend. Fill the container halfway with warm water, add just a drop of dishwashing liquid, and blast on high for 30 seconds. (More than a drop will foam all over the counter.) Rinse, wipe with a dishcloth, and dry with a soft cloth. To prevent buildup in the lid and inner lid cap, soak those pieces periodically in warm soapy water and use a small bottle brush, cotton swab, or toothpick to dislodge trapped particles. For stubborn stains, soak the carriage with a solution of vinegar, lemon juice, or baking soda, then wash and rinse again. For residual smells, use a mild solution of vinegar or vanilla extract.

Clean the base with a damp, soft cloth. A soft-bristled toothbrush can maneuver around the knobs and buttons. And pass a sponge over the unplugged cord to keep it from getting sticky and oily.

the spatula is queen

A pair of long-handled rubber spatulas, one with a broad scraper, the other thin and narrow, is essential to happy blending. The wide one works to shift foods mid-blending (with the machine off) and for bursting air pockets. The narrow one is invaluable after blending, for navigating around the blades to rescue every last morsel of your concoction. In the absence of a good spatula, I *have* been known to lick the last bits straight out of the carriage! But I wouldn't recommend this crass, codependent behavior to amateurs.

• • •

Now, choose your own blender adventure. Plug in your machine, head to the recipes (page 41), and blend up a storm! Or, read more about blending for health in the next chapter.

blendaholic picks

These are my picks this year. However, many companies are developing better technology, and the release of new models will widen the choices, raise standards, and (fingers crossed) lower prices.

BUDGET
Oster Beehive Osterizer Classic 4093 ($70)

You can't beat the price, and with some basic settings, this machine is proof that you don't need to spend a lot of money (and have elaborate functions) to get good results. This blender is particularly useful for smoothies and drinks. However, it won't give a silky-smooth consistency with nuts and seeds.

MID-RANGE
Breville Hemisphere Control BBL605XL ($200)
KitchenAid 5-Speed Diamond ($150)

The Breville is excellent value, with multiple settings, a timer, and lots of power out of a relatively quiet motor. The KitchenAid is also low on noise, with a base that locks down the container (a feature I love), and a decent amount of oomph. For most recipes, these machines are fabulous. However, they can struggle with thick blends and they lack the power to fully pulverize nuts, dates, and other hard ingredients.

IMMERSION ("HAND BLENDERS")
Breville Control Grip ($99)

Great for outfitting a small kitchen or for travelling, this machine is surprisingly powerful and comes in handy for one-pot cooking, pureeing vegetables and soups, and making skin creams and homemade cleaning products. The clever design ensures you don't scratch your pots, too. The whisk and chopper attachments and ergonomic trigger handle add up to great value.

---

note: I don't put containers or other blender parts in the dishwasher. Many manufacturers claim that parts are dishwasher safe, but my experience is that heat and fierce chemicals dull blades and warp lids. Corrosion can be an issue, too.

HIGH-SPEED
Vitamix 5200 ($450)

Blendtec makes very good high-speed blenders, and I'm a huge fan of the power of the top Omega models. But what distinguishes the Vitamix machines is the tamper (though some consumers find it annoying). This component lets you guide ingredients through the blades and burst air pockets with thick blends, all with the machine running. With both wet and dry containers, you can make smoothies, frozen desserts, nut butters, and steaming soups, as well as kneaded doughs and home-ground flours. Among Vitamix's several models, I prefer the 5200; its slender containers handle small and large blends equally well.

The multipurpose Thermomix is also an incredibly versatile high-speed machine, but with a retail price of around $1,500, it's cost-prohibitive for most of us.

SINGLE-SERVE
Nutribullet ($99)

An excellent option for travel, this compact machine is quite powerful. It's fantastic for making quick smoothies and dips and for chopping ingredients. However, it blends only small amounts and can easily overheat. If portability is not an issue, the full-sized Oster gives you more bang for your buck.

CHAPTER 2

healthy ideas to blend in

A few nutrition principles guide my food choices, which help me remain in a state of peak health and create a perfect blend day to day. Do you have to live the same way to enjoy the recipes in this book? No. However, as these ideas influence my recipes, they may help you better understand my approach. Including plenty of raw, soaked, and sprouted foods in your diet ensures a healthy dose of live enzymes and concentrated nutrients; consuming probiotic-rich foods boosts immunity; proper food combining aids optimum digestion; and remaining alkaline helps to strengthen and balance the body. I like to eat foods fresh and as close to their natural state as possible.

raw power

Raw fruits and vegetables; sprouted nuts, seeds, and grains; superfoods; and concentrated green powders all loom large in my diet and around my blender. Raw foods, which are never heated above 115°F (46°C), retain their full enzymatic and nutritional potential and are abundant in life-force energy. This food is in vibrant good health, and it will help keep us in the same state.

There is continued debate about the virtues of an all-raw diet. Some people abstain from cooked food altogether and thrive. Still, it's not for everyone and, I've discovered, not for me. When I adopted a strict raw diet for a year, I enjoyed a general boost in energy and wonderful cooling effects in hot weather. But my body cried out for a bit of heat

favorite raw foods

Fresh fruits and vegetables	Dips: guacamole, salsa, and pesto
Juices and smoothies	Sprouted crackers, breads, wraps, and pizzas
Kombucha and kefir	Puddings, ice creams, and desserts
Salads and cultured veggies	Superfood powders and purees
Savory and sweet soups	Sprouted-grain pilafs and sushi
Activated nuts, seeds, and butters	
Sun-dried and dehy-drated fruits and veggies	

and, in the colder months, I felt the pull of the strengthening quality of cooked foods.

Today I follow a diet high in raw foods but not exclusively raw. The proportion of cooked foods I eat varies with the seasons and changes as my needs do, depending on my stress levels, emotional state, physical activity, and overall health. For me, averaging about 75 percent raw food (that's eyeballing what I eat, not calculating calorie loads) is right. A different percentage may suit you. As a seasonal eater, I eat a summer diet that's almost completely raw, and then downshift to 50 percent raw when the weather turns colder.

As far as I'm concerned, there are no hard-and-fast rules, but raw foods unquestionably boost health. By making some of the raw recipes in the book, you may find the culinary benefits—flavor, texture, taste, aroma, and ease of preparation—just as appealing. Get raw daily, no question. Ideally, include something live in every meal. Here are some of the top reasons.

live enzymes and maximum nutrient potential

Enzymes are vital for facilitating every metabolic process in the body, from digestion to cell repair. Raw foods rich in live enzymes require less energy to digest, which leaves more for detoxification and regeneration. In fact, the more live enzymes you get, the more efficiently you derive nutrients from *all* the foods you eat.

Heating food to temperatures above 115°F (46°C) destroys these naturally occurring enzymes. So, more cooked food equals less enzyme action.

The body is about 70 percent water, and the food we eat must be liquefied for digestion. High-water-content raw foods, like cucumber, tomatoes, and watermelon, hydrate the body and require very little energy to be assimilated because they contain the water our bodies need to digest them. Cooking foods (even steaming and boiling) dries them out. Heavily cooked, processed, and animal-based foods are water-depleted and put a strain on the

l.s.o. (local, seasonal, organic) or grow

Choosing locally grown, organic produce whenever possible will give you healthier and tastier blends. This way you're eating in season, supporting your community, reducing your carbon footprint, and using foods that are free from synthetic pesticides and genetic modification. The best choice is to grow your own food. You can grow herbs easily, even with limited space.

digestive system. To be digested, they require additional water and that water has to come out of our reserves. Even mild dehydration has adverse effects, from hunger to sluggishness and fatigue.

I eat cooked foods with raw and hydrating co-stars, like a salad or sprouts, a dip or spread, cultured vegetables or pickles, or activated nuts and seeds to aid the digestive process with live enzymes.

cleansing power

Live foods are light and clean, and because they require less energy to digest, they pass through the body more quickly and efficiently than cooked foods, helping to rapidly eliminate toxins. This is particularly beneficial to the liver and colon. The intestine-cleansing properties of fiber are greatly reduced by cooking. Eating raw, alkaline foods that cool and cleanse the body is especially beneficial during times of illness.

increased energy

Every living organism contains and emits tiny physical units of light energy called *biophotons*. The foods we eat deliver this energy from the sun to our cells. The more of this life-force energy a food contains, the greater the potential for energy transfer. It only makes sense that living foods contain more biophotons than foods that have been cooked. More light in a food translates to greater nutrient density. The energy contained in raw foods can increase stamina, endurance, and overall vibrancy.

improved physical appearance

Because live foods are nutrient dense, contain water and live enzymes, take less time to digest, and have powerful cleansing properties, we look better as a result of eating them. A diet rich in raw foods translates to radiantly glowing skin, glossy hair, bright eyes, and strong nails, so we look our best. If that doesn't make you reach for a naked celery stick I don't know what will.

heightened senses and mental states

High consumption of raw foods can improve mental clarity, vision, hearing, reflexes, and sense of smell. Many people say that they experience, as I do, increased energy and a better and more stable mood from eating raw. I also find I need less sleep.

prevention of disease

In his book *Nutrition and Physical Degeneration*, Weston A. Price reported his findings after putting raw-food principles to the test. Price investigated the diets of numerous cultural groups around the world, from indigenous societies to highly urbanized and Westernized populations. What he found is that people who chiefly ate raw, unprocessed whole foods enjoyed enduring good health and greater resistance to degenerative ailments. Conversely, people who relied more on cooked and processed foods showed a higher propensity for infection and incidence of disease.

Highly processed foods are actually reconstituted dead foods devoid of any substantial nutrition. That these drastically modified foods taste any better than cardboard is largely a trick of chemical additives, including MSG and other artificial flavor enhancers, refined sugars, and bleached salts. Moreover, many convenience products, especially in the United States, are heavy in genetically modified ingredients, the safety of which remains very much in question.

washing

I wash all produce with a solution of 1 tablespoon baking soda plus 1 tablespoon apple cider vinegar or lemon juice per quart (liter) of water, and then rinse it well. Alternatively, you can peel food, but much of the goodness in fruits and veggies lies in the skins or just beneath.

raw foods taste great

Raw foods are light, clean, fresh, vibrant, bursting with flavor, vivid with color, and can be prepared in a diversity of interesting and satisfying ways (that don't have to take a lot of time). Chopped, shredded, diced, juiced, blended, or gently dehydrated, live foods can be as simple as veggie sticks with pesto or salsa; quick juices, shakes, and smoothies; or a million different kinds of salads and collard wraps, gazpacho-style savory soups, and sweet fruit soups. Or you can go for something more adventurous and prepare raw no-pasta pasta dishes (see pages 128 and 136), crackers, bread, sushi, or sprouted grain dishes. Raw puddings (see page 159), pies (see pages 168 and 170), and ice creams are delicious, and are as easy to make as "blend and chill." Don't overlook live fermented foods, such as kombucha and kefir (see page 30), and cultured vegetables (see page 84). Yes, there is a *lot* more to raw food than wilted lettuce leaves and dry, warped carrot sticks.

To maximize both nutrient power and pleasure, I soak many live foods. This unlocks their full potential, helps them blend better, and yields the best results in flavor and texture. Soaking is a game-changer (see page 21).

superfoods

Packed with vitamins, minerals, and antioxidants, superfoods are easy to incorporate into smoothies.

Most seem ludicrously expensive, but they're so nutritionally dense that the cost per serving isn't high. **Goji berries** are a silent star, with a complete amino acid profile, balanced fat composition, and mineral-rich personality. Their tart, sometimes bitter flavor blends into the Creamy Orange C (page 57) all but undetected. **Camu berries** are the number-one natural source of vitamin C. **Mulberries** are one of the top sources of anti-aging antioxidants. Their mildly sweet flavor complements berries, citrus, and vanilla. **Maqui berries** have the highest known level of antioxidants and a mild flavor that is easily mixed with other foods. **Açaí** has a delicate flavor that can be teased out by bananas, dates, berries, and creamy milks. Low in sugar but rich in amino acids and omegas 3, 6, and 9, açaí is crammed with antioxidants. I add maqui berries and açaí to the Antioxidant Avenger (page 51). **Pomegranate** also contains significant antioxidants (three times that of green tea), as well as powerful antiviral and antibacterial properties. **Cacao** hauls a truckload of antioxidants (twice as many as açaí) and claims the title of highest-magnesium food. It *is* a stimulant, but is a calcium- and iron-rich chocolate fix. For increased energy and adrenal support without the stimulant component, a teaspoon (any more can be unpalatable) of **maca powder** is the ticket. A light touch also yields the best results with chlorophyll-rich green powders such as **spirulina**, **chlorella**, and **wheatgrass** (see Minty Green Gluttony, page 63). **Flaxseeds**, **hemp seeds**, and **chia seeds** are chock-full of nutrients, antioxidants, essential fatty acids, fiber, and protein and feature in several of my recipes.

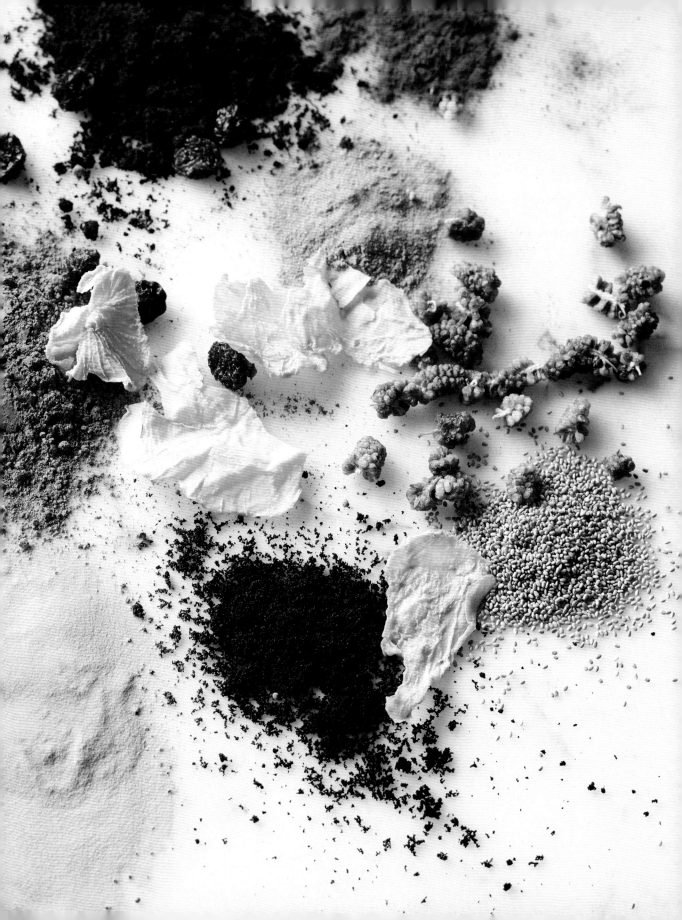

soak and sprout, never doubt

I was introduced to the magical health practice of soaking nuts, seeds, and grains by Sally Fallon's book *Nourishing Traditions*. Before Fallon made me a believer, I'd scarf down these foods as they came, and soon be nursing a tummy ache and feeling tired and bloated. At the time, I thought I was facing eternal deprivation. My motto now? "Be a soaker, not a bloater!"

to soak or not to soak? that isn't a question

Nuts, seeds, and grains are brilliant products of nature that contain inhibitors (like armor) to prevent germination until the conditions are right and their survival is ensured. However, these protective agents also act as enzyme inhibitors, waging a war in our digestive systems and compromising our health. Other inconvenient warriors lurking in the outer layers of whole grains include antinutrients (such as phytates) that work like shields. These suckers can inhibit our absorption of nutrients like iron, calcium, copper, zinc, and magnesium. Should we surrender and switch to white refined staples (with much of the nutrition stripped out) in order to win the battle? No, we roll up our sleeves, jump into the trenches, and get wet. Kapow—battle won!

---

note: When cooking soaked grains, use about half the water you would to cook unsoaked. A one-to-one ratio (by volume) of water to soaked grain is usually sufficient to cook them to al dente. When using soaked grains in recipes, start with half the liquid called for, and gradually add more until you reach the desired consistency.

---

soaking is quick and easy

Soaking only *sounds* like a lot of work and a drag. Slow-soaking for nutritional benefit takes a little advance planning, but just a few minutes of hands-on time. Quick-soaking serves for strictly culinary purposes. In both cases, the payoff is well worth the effort.

Foods require different soaking times for full germination (see the chart on page 24). As a general rule with nuts: the harder the nut, the longer the soak. Long-soak nuts (almonds, pistachios, and hazelnuts) need at least 8 hours. Medium-soak nuts (pecans, walnuts, and Brazil nuts) are oilier and swell up quickly, so require less soaking time. Short-soak nuts (cashews, macadamias, and pine nuts) get the briefest bath. Oversoaking these creamier nuts breaks down their precious and flavorful oils.

five good reasons to soak

Improves digestion: Soaking raw nuts, seeds, and whole grains in warm acidulated or salted water simulates the ideal moist germinating conditions these foods wait for in nature, essentially tricking the food into sprouting, which neutralizes enzyme inhibitors.

Unlocks nutrients: Soaking activates the full nutrient potential of food. The potency of vitamins like A, C, and B get a boost, proteins become more available, and live enzymes are released.

Produces better flavor and texture: Soaking softens food, making it easier to blend. Hydrated nuts, seeds, and dried fruits liquefy more completely, even in high-speed machines. The silky, creamy consistency you get by soaking nuts before blending into soups and smoothies isn't achievable with unsoaked nuts. Similarly, soaking dates for smoothies and sweets, and sun-dried tomatoes for raw sauces yields the best results.

Reduces cooking time: There are culinary benefits to soaking outside the blender, too. Soaked grains cook more quickly, and soaked brown rice, when cooked, gets fluffy like its popular white counterpart.

Prevents blender wear and tear: Soaking hard and fibrous foods means less labor for the motor.

soaking for better health

The easiest way to incorporate long soaking into your lifestyle is to soak right before bed, then rinse, drain, and dry upon rising. Alternatively, soak in the morning to use at night. If you're combining foods in a recipe, as you might do to make a mixed-nut milk, soak ingredients separately, and then blend (see page 26). Here are my basic instructions for soaking.

1. Soak your food in a glass or ceramic container. Fully cover it with a solution of warm water, natural salt (see page 38), and apple cider vinegar or lemon juice. I generally use two parts water to one part food by volume; per quart or liter of water, I add ½ teaspoon of salt and 1 teaspoon of lemon juice or vinegar. So, to soak one cup of almonds, I'd add ¼ teaspoon salt and ½ teaspoon acid to 2 cups (480ml) of water, and immerse the nuts in the mixture.

2. Cover the bowl with a thin dish towel so the food can breathe and let stand at room temperature for the directed period (see chart on page 24). It's normal to see a few dubious nuts, seeds, or grains floating on the surface, possibly rancid. Discard those. You'll also notice particles and a murky film on the surface and sediment on the bottom. These are the anti-nutrients that soaking has drawn out; better in the bowl than in our bodies!

3. Rinse thoroughly. Empty the contents of the bowl into a colander or strainer, rinse the bowl, and then place the food back in. Refill the bowl with clean water, fully submerging the food, then swish the contents around, strain, and rinse again.

Freshly soaked nuts and seeds are ideal for immediate use in milks, creams, smoothies, soups, and desserts. Alternatively, dehydrate soaked items (see instructions below) for use later as snacks, or to make butters, crusts, and flours. Soaked grains can be cooked or used in recipes, or dehydrated. Alternatively, you can sprout soaked nuts, seeds, and grains (see opposite page). Soaked foods like dried fruits and vegetables have to be used immediately.

dehydrating

If you're not using nuts, seeds, and grains immediately after soaking, dehydrate them. Drying foods in an electric dehydrator (which works at low temperatures so raw foods retain their live enzymes) allows you to preserve activated foods for use in a variety of recipes.

To dehydrate, spread out your soaked foods on the dehydrator's mesh-screened trays and dry for 12 to 48 hours at a setting no higher than 115°F (46°C)

---

soaking foods for blending

Nuts, seeds, and grains: To soak the fast way, place the food in a glass or ceramic container, cover with boiling water and let soak for 10 minutes or more. This softens foods quickly for culinary use, but has no nutritional benefit because live enzymes are destroyed. Drain thoroughly, discard the soaking liquid, and rinse. To soak the slow way, for both nutritional *and* culinary benefits, refer to page 24 for soak times and see above for instructions. The soaking liquid should be discarded as it contains antinutrients (toxic inhibitors) that are not beneficial for health.

Dates: Pit and chop, cover with either the base liquid in your recipe or with water. Soak for at least 30 minutes and up to 8 hours. Add both the soaking liquid and dates to your recipe (to add sweetness and flavor) or drain the water and add only the dates.

Other dried fruits and vegetables: With small fruits and vegetables like raisins, apricots, prunes, cherries, blueberries, goji berries, camu berries, mulberries, and sun-dried tomatoes, place the food in a glass or ceramic container and fill with either the base liquid in your recipe or just enough water to cover. Soak for 15 minutes to 1 hour, then drain.

---

to preserve the live enzymes. Most manuals come with instructions for specific foods. Seeds typically dry best at about 100°F (38°C) and nuts at 115°F (46°C). Allow the food to dry and cool completely (it'll get crunchy) before sealing in an airtight container. If it holds any residual moisture, it will quickly make friends with some mold. To avoid this, leave the lid off the container for a few hours before sealing it up. If you don't have a dehydrator, you *can* use a regular baking sheet and dry on the lowest setting of your oven. But keep in mind that even a standard oven's warm setting is well above 115°F (46°C), more than hot enough to kill live enzymes.

buying a dehydrator

I highly recommend investing in a dehydrator. Ideally, you want a machine with an adjustable thermostat (which allows you to control the internal temperature) and a fan to ensure even and efficient drying. If the temperature is too high, enzymes are destroyed; if it's too low, the food is prey to bacteria and spoilage, and takes a long time to dry. Basic stackable machines without temperature controls are undesirable, as the air can't circulate effectively. These machines also dry from the bottom up, so you have to keep rotating the trays. Another feature that's nice (while not essential) is an automatic timer, which makes dehydrating more convenient. Also, consider the capacity, which is a matter of personal preference.

The brand I prefer is Excalibur. The company makes 4-tray, 5-tray, and 9-tray machines, with or without timers. Available in a variety of colors and retailing between $130 and $400, they have options to accommodate most situations. I own the 9-tray model with timer so I can make large batches of kale chips (see page 80) and activated nuts and seeds. It's also worth purchasing the nonstick sheets ($10 to $15 each) for making fruit leathers (page 81), wraps, cookies, and desserts.

sprouting

Sprouted (activated) foods are widely available at health food stores. But why hand over stashes of cash when it's so easy to make your own? Sprouted live foods are some of the most nutritionally dense foods and I include them in my diet as much as possible.

Sprouting *does* require patience and attention. I start soaking the foods I plan to sprout just before I go to bed, so they're ready to go into sprouting jars in the morning. Getting them ready takes just a couple of minutes. Then it's only a matter of checking on them, and making sure they stay hydrated. On a sunny windowsill, they're easy to manage while you do other things.

Note that most seeds, legumes, and grains *will* sprout a tail but some won't. Most nuts will not physically sprout. A raw nut or seed may not have been cooked, technically, but still may have been irradiated, pasteurized, or subjected to heat to crack its hard shell. Almonds that aren't truly raw will activate nutritionally with soaking, but won't sprout. (Refer to the chart on page 24 for specific sprouting characteristics).

It's important to note that sprouts are susceptible to contamination, which can cause bacterial growth such as *E. coli*, resulting in food poisoning. When preparing your sprouts, always wash your hands thoroughly, keep sprouting equipment and kitchen surfaces clean to avoid cross contamination, and consume within a couple of days, straight out of the fridge. When purchasing commercial sprouts, always source fresh products from a reputable supplier.

soaking to sprout

Most sprouts will keep in the fridge for two to three days. Use them in raw salads, sandwiches, and wraps, or to top soups and stews. They can be pretty fabulous in smoothies, too. Turn the page to read my basic instructions for sprouting.

1. Soak your goods in a mason jar with a flat metal lid and a ring top. Remove the lid from the ring and use it as a guide to cut a piece of breathable mesh or cheesecloth to cover the opening of the jar. Place the food you want to sprout into the jar, only about one-third full, and fill the jar with warm water and a bit of natural salt (1/4 teaspoon per cup of water). Close the jar with the breathable cover and the ring. Let the jar rest on a counter top for the desired time (see chart, at right).

2. To drain, remove the ring and the mesh, pour out the water, and then fill the jar with fresh, warm water. Replace the flat metal lid and secure it with the ring. Rinse the food well by shaking the jar. Drain and repeat. After draining the water for the second time, refit the mesh, close the jar with the ring, and lay the jar down at an angle, so excess water drains out. Leave the jar on its side to sit in natural light on a counter top or windowsill to drain. Repeat the rinsing and draining every few hours, or at least twice a day. Make sure you angle the jar to drain off excess liquid and that you keep it in the sunlight until the food is fully sprouted.

3. Most foods sprout in 1 to 4 days (see chart, at right). Sprouts vary in length from 1/8 inch to 2 inches (3mm to 5cm), and not all will show signs of green. When the sprouts are ready, do a final rinse, drain thoroughly, and tilt the jar for further drainage until the sprouts are completely dry. (If they're damp, they'll spoil.) When they're dry to the touch, replace the flat metal lid, secure with the ring, and store the jar in the fridge.

Including soaked and sprouted foods in your diet not only maximizes nutrient availability and expands culinary pleasure, but also encourages the proliferation of friendly bacteria in the digestive system, which boosts immunity. Consuming these foods in conjunction with cultured foods is a winning strategy for fostering a healthy internal balance.

soaking and sprouting chart

Food	Soaking Time (hours)	Sprouting Time (days)
Adzuki beans	8 to 12	4
Almonds	8 to 12	No sprouting, or 3 days (if truly raw)
Amaranth	8	1 to 3
Barley	6	2
Black beans	8 to 12	3
Brazil nuts	3	No sprouting
Buckwheat	6	2 to 3
Cashews	2 to 4	No sprouting
Chickpeas/ garbanzo beans	8	2 to 3
Flaxseeds	1/2	No sprouting
Hazelnuts	8 to 12	No sprouting
Kamut	7	2 to 3
Lentils	7	2 to 3
Macadamias	2	No sprouting
Millet	5	12 hours
Mung beans	8 to 12	4
Oat groats	6	2 to 3
Pecans	6	No sprouting
Pistachios	8	No sprouting
Pumpkin seeds	8	3
Quinoa	5	2 to 3
Radish seeds	8 to 12	3 to 4
Sesame seeds	8	2 to 3
Sunflower seeds	8	12 to 24 hours
Walnuts	4	No sprouting
Wheat berries	7	3 to 4
Wild rice	9	3 to 5

cooking sprouts

Some health authorities recommend cooking
sprouts to reduce the risk of foodborne illness.
I consume sprouts raw, to benefit from their
live enzymes and nutrient density, and have
never had an issue. You decide yourself on the
responsible choice for you and your family.

milk it, baby!

My motto is "If you can blend it, you can milk it." Almonds, cashews, macadamias, Brazil nuts, hazelnuts, pecans, pistachios, coconut, soybeans, hemp seeds, pumpkin seeds, sunflower seeds, sesame seeds, sacha inchi seeds, flaxseeds, quinoa, millet, rice, and oats can all be liquefied with water and turned into plant-based milks.

Homemade milks that use raw ingredients contain live enzymes and nutrients and are free of additives, preservatives, and hormones. Moreover, you can completely control the integrity of the product: the quality of the ingredients and sugar levels, as well as the texture. Another bonus is that, unlike commercial milks, your homemade milk can be made more digestible via soaking. I source organic, non-GMO ingredients wherever possible.

milking is easy!

Don't be intimidated by the concept—milking is *so* easy, and requires neither chewing a cud nor being hooked up to a machine by a guy in overalls. It's as simple as "soak, blend, strain, and serve." These milks are loaded with nutrients and are delicious! For nutritional diversity, I make a different variety every day, and use many of these milks (strained) in my recipes.

mix and flavor

Combine two types of nuts or seeds for tasty variation. I *love* almond-hazelnut milk. (Soak the components separately before blending.) Add flavorings like vanilla, raw cacao, cocoa, or carob, and fresh fruit such as strawberries. Spices like cinnamon, nutmeg, and cardamom also keep things interesting.

don't forget the soak

I soak all nuts, seeds, and grains for milking. This improves digestibility and softens ingredients to help them liquefy better (see page 29 for soaking times). The soak is especially important if you don't have a high-speed blender.

to strain or not to strain?

This is a matter of preference. You can make milks in *any* blender. But you'll get the milkiest results with a high-speed machine. With a regular blender, if you're after that silky dairy consistency, you'll need to strain. Some milks, such as almond and Brazil nut, require straining no matter which type of blender you use. While unstrained milks are wonderful for fiber and nutrition, most of my recipes calling for milks will benefit from the texture of a strained blend.

To strain milks, invest a few dollars in a filtration bag, also known as a nut-milk bag. Purchase these at health food stores or online (see page 208). These reusable bags will last, provided you wash them thoroughly and let them air-dry immediately after use. But you can start milking right away even without one. A piece of sheer hosiery works wonders!

store or make more

I make a batch of my basic milk recipe (see page 28) every day. It yields 2 to 3 cups of strained milk. Unless you have a large family or use a lot of milk, this is a good amount to keep on hand. Homemade milks can be stored in the fridge for 2 or 3 days.

freeze your milk

Pour leftover milk into ice-cube trays, freeze, and store for later. Frozen milks (see page 55) make smoothies and soups creamy and can be defrosted for use on cereal.

commercial milks

The quality of commercial milks varies greatly. Ingredient lists speak volumes about the integrity of the products. Look for milks that use organic, non-GMO ingredients and have little in the way of additives, preservatives, stabilizers, thickeners, and sweeteners. Fresh is best. However, this is not always possible. When a recipe calls for unsweetened milk, a commercial version of the type of milk specified (if one's available) can be used instead of homemade.

Use this basic recipe as a general guide for making your own nut milks at home. Refer to the chart (opposite page) for soak times and ingredient ratios.

sweetened milk

1 cup of your chosen raw nut, grain, or seed

Water, preferably filtered (see chart, opposite page)

1 teaspoon alcohol-free vanilla extract

2 to 3 tablespoons sweetener (maple syrup, coconut sugar, or raw agave nectar); 3 or 4 chopped, pitted, and soaked (see page 22) dates; or 5 to 10 drops alcohol-free liquid stevia

1 tablespoon coconut oil, in liquid form (optional, for texture)

1 tablespoon sunflower lecithin (optional, to emulsify and add creaminess)

Pinch of natural salt (optional, to bring out flavors)

Measure out the nut, seed, or grain and then soak according to the soaking instructions on page 22. Drain and rinse thoroughly and transfer to the blender. Add the water (see chart, opposite page), vanilla, sweetener, coconut oil, and lecithin. Blend on high for 1 to 2 minutes, until fully liquefied. (If your blender heats the milk, don't be alarmed—the heat won't harm it). Tweak sweetener to taste. Enjoy unstrained, or strain by placing a filtration bag over a container, pouring the milk into the bag, twisting the bag closed, and gently squeezing it to pass the liquid through. Store in the fridge for 2 to 3 days. It's normal for the mixture to separate. Just shake or blend again before using.

variation: unsweetened milk Blend the soaked nut, seed, or grain of your choice with the required amount of water and then strain. Omit the sweetener and other additions.

variation: almond milk "kefir" Blend 1 cup of soaked almonds with 7 cups of water and strain. Transfer the mixture to a glass or ceramic bowl and gently stir in 1 teaspoon of probiotic powder (or the contents of 4 capsules) with a wooden spoon. (Metal implements will damage the delicate probiotics.) Cover the bowl with a breathable cloth and let stand at room temperature (70°F/21°C) for 12 hours (longer in a cold room; wrap the bowl with a towel to insulate for better results). The cultured milk is ready when the mixture has a yellow tinge, a thick layer of skin on the top, and a fermented smell like yogurt. If there is just a thin layer and not much aroma, it's not quite done. Gently skim this kefir-cream off with a spoon and keep for use in smoothies and puddings. Strain the liquid. Store in a sealed glass container in the fridge for up to 1 week.

To make subsequent batches, reserve 1/2 cup of kefir to culture the next batch. After making three more batches this way, start over with probiotic powder.

note: Milk and water kefir are traditionally cultured using kefir grains. But these grains can be difficult to work with, often contain dairy or dairy by-products, and are easily contaminated. The easiest way to get consistent results with plant-based milks, and accurately measure the degree of colonization, is to use probiotic powder. While not technically "kefir," the liquid is still a probiotic-rich food.

milking cheat sheet

In general, a one-to-three ratio (by volume) of food to water yields good results for homemade milks. For rich milks, I start with two-thirds of the water called for and gradually add more to get the taste and consistency I like. (The exception is flaxseeds, which absorb a lot of water.) Don't waste the leftover pulp. It's fantastic for making crackers, cookies, and crusts. Or mix it with coconut, almond, apricot, or avocado oil to make body scrubs.

	Food	Soaking Time (hours)	Water	Strain	Yield
Almonds, whole	1 cup/160g	8 to 12	3 cups/720ml	Yes	3 cups/720ml
Brazil nuts	1 cup/140g	3	3 cups/720ml	Yes	2 1/2 cups/600ml
Brown Rice	1/2 cup/170g (cooked*)	8 to 12	2 cups/480ml	Yes	2 cups/480ml
Cashews	1 cup/140g	2 to 4	3 cups/720ml	No	3 cups/720ml
Coconut, raw meat	1 cup/180g	0	3 cups/720ml coconut water	No	4 cups/960ml
Flaxseeds	1/4 to 1/2 cup/ 42 to 84g, to taste	1/2	6 cups/1.4l	Yes	6 cups/1.4l
Hazelnuts	1 cup/150g	8 to 12	2 cups/480ml	Yes	2 cups/480ml
Hemp seeds	1 cup/140g	No Soak	3 cups/720ml	Yes	2 1/2 cups/600ml
Macadamias	1 cup/140g	2	3 cups/720ml	No	3 cups/720ml
Millet	1 cup/174g (cooked*)	5	4 cups/960ml	Yes	3 1/2 cups/840ml
Oats, steel-cut	1 cup/100g	1 to 8	3 cups/720ml	Yes/Twice	3 cups/720ml
Pecans	1 cup/110g	6	3 cups/720ml	No	3 cups/720ml
Pistachios	1 cup/120g	8	3 cups/720ml	Yes	3 1/2 cups/840ml
Pumpkin seeds	1 cup/140g	8	3 cups/720ml	Yes	2 1/2 cups/600ml
Quinoa	1 cup/170g (cooked*)	5	3 cups/720ml	Yes	2 1/2 cups/600ml
Sacha inchi seeds	1 1/2 cups/225g	8	2 1/2 cups/600ml	Yes	3 cups/720ml
Sesame seeds, hulled	1 cup/140g	8	3 cups/720ml	Yes	3 1/2 cups/840ml
Soy beans, dried	1 1/2 cups/210g (cooked*)	11	3 1/2 cups/840ml	Yes	3 1/2 cups/840ml
Sunflower seeds	1 cup/140g	8	3 cups/720ml	Yes	2 1/2 cups/600ml

* To make milks with ingredients that must be cooked first: begin by soaking (see page 22), then cook, add water, blend, and strain.

probiotic is proactive

Regular consumption of probiotic-rich (fermented) foods is a boon to health. Our inner ecosystem is complex and delicate, and home to hundreds of species of microorganisms—both hostile and friendly—constantly battling for dominance. When we're healthy, the life-affirming bacteria (the most common are **lactobacillus** and **bifidus**) are strong enough to outmaneuver their nefarious counterparts.

Probiotics replenishment is vital for maintaining a balanced inner ecology to support overall health. Foods containing probiotics help build mineral-rich alkaline blood, are essential for the assimilation of protein, greatly improve digestion, help fight disease, and are cleansing.

However, we're all busy and barraged by influences that make maintaining this balance a challenge. Environmental pollutants and chemicals, poor air and water quality, pesticides, hormonal changes due to pregnancy, the use of birth control in women, preservatives in food, and the use of antibiotics throw our intestinal flora and fauna out of whack. Emotional and physical stress contributes to the imbalance and can make processed and fast foods an attractive and easy choice.

When our inner chemistry is out of balance, disease-causing bacteria feed on the healthy nutrients in our bodies and release toxic wastes that weaken our defenses and allow tenacious colonies of yeast and other fungi to take systemic control.

To be proactive about my health, I make a point of eating foods rich in probiotics as part of an alkaline diet low in sugar and high in essential vitamins and minerals.

My picks for natural probiotic replenishers are kefir (I favor coconut water and almond milk varieties) and cultured vegetables. To assist, I call on high-quality powdered probiotics supplements and consume prebiotic foods (those that encourage the proliferation of probiotics and help sustain healthy digestive flora). My favorite prebiotics are fresh vegetables from both land and sea, and sprouted foods (see page 23).

note: Probiotic powder features as an optional ingredient in some of my smoothies (where the taste is undetectable) to help balance sugars. The really potent probiotics that I favor require refrigeration. I avoid capsules because the gel cap is not easily digestible, but if that's what you use, simply break the shell to release the powder. I consume $^1/_2$ teaspoon every day.

kefir

Kefir is widely available at health food stores. Read labels to ensure the integrity of the product, as many brands include processed sugar and additives. Making your own kefir lets you control both quality and flavor.

You can turn any kind of milk, coconut water, or plain water into kefir by adding a culture starter or kefir grains and some natural sugar to feed the organisms. Probiotic powder—technically not the same as kefir culture—is an easy-to-use, vegan alternative that yields uniform results (see note, above). How much time a kefir needs to develop depends on the base ingredient and the starter used.

I prefer coconut water kefir—a brilliant blood builder and energy booster that's high in protein and loaded with alkaline minerals. It also supplies lots of vitamin B_{12}, which is essential to the formation of red blood cells that fight disease, improves digestion, and tones the intestines. It can also improve vision, strengthen hair and nails, dry up moles and warts, smooth skin, and fade skin spots.

As a long-time fan of kefir, I can back up many of its claims. With its tart flavor, it can be an acquired taste. I enjoy the bite, and I think of coconut water kefir as a healthy spritzer or champagne cocktail—without the hangover! But it is **potent**. Just a half cup in the morning and half cup at night before bed (or a cup mixed with low-sugar fruit and alcohol-free stevia) is all you need. To get the most bang for your buck, drink your kefir right before bed, so the probiotics can settle in and have a colonization party. Less really is more. Yes, I have overdone it, and spent more time in the company of our porcelain friend than I care to remember.

live-cultured vegetables

These are powerhouse foods, and I include a portion with every meal. These enzyme-rich foods are basically shredded raw veggies (cabbage, carrots, beets, onion, garlic, herbs, and others) fermented at room temperature to produce a growth of healthy bacteria. (Think sauerkraut minus the salt, pasteurization, and bratwurst; or kimchi minus the fiery Korean chile.) There's no need to add a culture; the foods will do the job on their own.

A lot of people turn their noses up at the thought of eating anything with pungent punch. *Fermented*? Yuck. But these mineral-dense vegetables are tender, tangy, and delicious, and offer novel flavor combinations. Alkaline forming, they greatly assist with digestion (particularly of protein), help eliminate toxins, and rejuvenate cells and tissues. They also combine well with proteins and starches.

Making cultured vegetables takes just 30 or 40 minutes' prep. After a few days, or up to a week, of fermentation, they're ready. A delicious accompaniment to other dishes, these vegetables are cheaper than probiotic powders and are much more effective. (For my favorite recipe, see page 84).

---

note: Cultured foods are wonderful options for people with a sensitive digestive tract and a compromised immune system because the sugars have been pre-digested and converted into lactic acid, making the food gentle on the body. Doctors recommend consuming probiotics after any course of antibiotics to help restore healthy ecology.

---

cayenne

This is the easiest way to boost your probiotic potential. Cayenne pepper is not probiotic-rich but probiotic friendly. It stimulates the secretion of hydrochloric acid, which plays a critical role in digestion and encourages those great bacteria. It also adds a fabulous kick to dishes. For all of these reasons, you'll see this ground hot pepper in several of my recipes.

Mineral-rich probiotic foods strengthen the entire body. Improper food combining, however, promotes fermentation and feeds the unfriendly bacteria and yeast, all of which are counterproductive to probiotic replenishment.

food combine to really shine

Food combining is an approach to eating that works on the premise that our bodies can optimally digest only one concentrated food at a time. Concentrated foods are typically defined as starches and proteins—basically, anything other than fruits and vegetables. Digestion of starches (grains, potatoes, and many other roots) calls for alkaline conditions, whereas the enzymes that digest protein thrive in an acidic environment. If we eat a starch and a protein together, we're essentially asking our digestive systems to be alkaline and acidic at the same time. Unfortunately, Western menu combos tend to do just that. Eating a good old meat-and-potatoes meal calls in digestive processes that neutralize each other. Neither the meat nor the potatoes gets handled effectively, leading to fermentation, which feeds yeast and fungus. This chain reaction disrupts the digestion of *all* the foods we eat. We may be unaware of what's going on, but we experience the impact as bloating, flatulence, and indigestion. I certainly did. Once a stereotypical vegetarian who eats too many lentils, I was the butt of a lot of jokes. My aunt made a point, annually no less, of hunting down a fart-themed birthday card for me and voicing the family's collective hope of a cure. TMI? Perhaps, but an all-too-familiar story. Proper food combining not only eradicated my gaseous rumblings, it also improved my assimilation and absorption of nutrients, giving me more energy.

Ever feel tired and lethargic after you eat? Well, digestion is like an athletic endeavor and can demand more energy than strenuous exercise. If we help it along, we don't feel zapped. Poor digestion leaves less energy for vitality. Worse, it puts a strain on the liver, our all-important regenerative and detox organ, which we want working at its best. (It's no accident that it's called the *live*-er.)

While not every recipe in this book is anchored in food-combining principles, I do employ them in my daily life and food choices. Some excellent books (see page 210) offer comprehensive systems; however, I believe in bio-individuality and in building habits based on experience as well as on received information. I pay attention to how foods combine, but I'm not dogmatic. I cook and dine out with as much abandon as the next person. Rigid rules just aren't much fun. Keeping a few basics in mind, you may want to experiment.

Food combining isn't *quite* as simple as distinguishing concentrated foods from everything else. There are also subcategories of food that combine best with certain others. I'll walk through the guidelines *I* follow. My mixes and matches are merely suggestions and observations. Find what works for you.

some people are just fruity till noon

Food-combining purists say that fruit is best eaten on its own. Your liver works hardest to eliminate toxins between midnight and midday. Digesting fruit doesn't require action by the liver, so to support optimal cleansing, traditional food combiners consume fruit alone in the a.m. hours. Fruit is a great replenisher of fluids after a night of rest and moves quickly from the stomach into the small intestine. A fruit breakfast leaves the stomach ready for a more varied lunch.

I *do* ease into my gastronomic day, but I'm not a food-combining fundamentalist. First thing, I hydrate by drinking two glasses of warm water with fresh lemon juice (using a straw, to spare the enamel on my teeth). In addition to giving me an alkalinity bump (lemon becomes alkaline when digested), this stimulates the peristaltic movement of the digestive system—sending the message that there's food coming soon. Next, I drink a few more glasses of water containing liquid chlorophyll to build my blood (see page 36). If I'm stressed, I'll have some diluted black currant juice for an antioxidant boost to the adrenals. Once I'm hungry,

I sip my way through a big green alkaline smoothie (a combination of spinach, cucumber, coconut, avocado, lime, and stevia is a favorite) or tuck into a fruit salad or parfait. And tomatoes, cucumbers, and avocados are fruits, too; a morning salad is a good breakfast and keeps the sugar down.

But, this kind of morning regime isn't for everyone. You can get *really* hungry, particularly when you first start eating this way. And some people need to start the day with foods that deliver more heat and sustenance. If that's how you roll, try having fruit or a green smoothie and then waiting for 30 minutes (if your breakfast includes bananas, pears, or avocados, make it 45) before eating something more.

As a general rule, sour or acidic fruits (grapefruits, kiwis, and strawberries) can be combined with "protein fats" such as avocado, coconut, coconut kefir, and sprouted nuts and seeds. Both acid fruits and sub-acid fruits like apples, grapes, and pears can be eaten with cheeses; and vegetable fruits (avocados, cucumbers, tomatoes, and peppers) can be eaten with fruits, vegetables, starches, and proteins. I've also found that apples combine well with raw vegetables. Leafy greens (spinach, kale, collard greens), along with the vegetable fruits noted above, are my go-to staples. They are the magic foods that combine well with every food on the planet. I blend them together in green smoothies, cold soups, and salads. As melons digest faster than any other food, a food-combining motto is "melon on its own or leave it alone." I find I tolerate melon with other fruits, but discover what works best for you.

Unfortunately, sweet fruits do not combine well with concentrated starches and proteins, which typically take three to five hours to digest. Fruit is often recommended for cleansing, but when it's trapped in the longer digestive cycle of concentrated food, fruit ferments and produces acid and alcohol, which feeds yeast, fungus, and bacteria. After you eat a starch or protein meal, it's best to wait at least five hours to have fruit.

proteins with no-starch and sea is for me

Upon receiving concentrated proteins (meat, fish, eggs, tofu, tempeh), the stomach cranks up the hydrochloric acid and the protein-digesting enzyme pepsin—as noted earlier, not a good environment for digestion of starches. Proteins are best combined with non-starchy vegetables such as spinach, carrots, onions, and broccoli, or with sea vegetables (nori, kombu, wakame, arame, hijiki, and dulse), all of which happily digest in both a protein or starch-friendly environment. Leave 4 to 5 hours between a protein meal and a starch meal.

starches with no-starch and sea is also key

Non-grain starches like potatoes, corn, fresh peas, winter squashes, and artichokes can be combined with rice, quinoa, millet, buckwheat, amaranth, and other grains. These starchy foods also work well with non-starchy vegetables like leafy greens and sea vegetables. Classic duos like vegetable curry with grains, pasta with tomato-based sauce, and baked potatoes with salad or coleslaw go together not only for flavor and texture, but also for health reasons.

combining protein fats with no-starch and sea means glee

The protein fats include avocado, nuts, seeds, cheeses, and olives. These combine best with sea vegetables and other non-starchy vegetables and with acid fruits. I put avocados in green smoothies, use them with nuts and seeds to make desserts, and serve them in salads with non-starchy vegetables.

protein starches in moderation or . . .

Legumes, classified as "protein starches" (both a protein and a starch), are difficult to digest. Soaking beans or dried peas with a strip of kombu helps alleviate some gas. Protein starches can still be problematic and are best kept to a minimum. Combine them with non-starchy vegetables, including sea vegetables.

This may all sound like a hassle, but there *are* flavorful foods that combine well with everything: vegetable fruits and leafy greens. Non-starchy foods, including sea vegetables, also combine well with most things. So food combining is less restrictive than it seems. It calls for a bit of thinking (and rethinking) about how and when and what you eat—but it's not a matter of "don't eat this, or this, or this." Once you give it a try, you'll probably have a hard time believing how good you feel. Similarly, including more alkaline foods is easier, and tastier, than it first appears.

---

note: A major reason that processed foods have so many adverse side effects is that most contain sugar. Sugar combines well with . . . nothing. So, the less of it you consume, the sweeter your life will be.

alkaline angels

Reading *The pH Miracle* by Dr. Robert O. Young introduced me to the extraordinary health benefits of alkalinity. When my partner, Scott, was diagnosed with thyroid cancer, Dr. Young contributed greatly to restoring his health by prescribing an alkaline diet. Since Scott and I voiced the audiobook editions of *The pH Miracle* series, we've heard from hundreds of listeners who've adopted alkaline-boosting practices and report great health improvements as well.

The vital balance between acidity and alkalinity in our internal chemistry *rules* our bodies. The fluids of different regions within us have varying optimal pH readings, but the average ideal pH for our blood is slightly alkaline: 7.365.

But here's the rub. The human body is alkaline in form, but acidic in function. The body must be in an alkaline state to operate at its best, but the by-products of all of its functions are acidic. So, we need to help our bodies stay alkaline.

what is pH?

The abbreviation is for "potential hydrogen," the measure of acidity or alkalinity. The pH scale runs from 0 to 14, with a reading below 7 being acidic and above 7 being alkaline or "basic." The pH scale, like the Richter scale, is logarithmic. Each number up or down represents a tenfold difference, so a pH of 9 is not a *bit* more alkaline than one of 8, but ten times more.

The right pH is absolutely critical for optimum health. Innumerable factors, including pollutants, physical and psychological stress, negative emotions, prescription and non-prescription drugs, all push our bodies toward acidity. Our bodies are clever and keep a reserve of "alkaline buffers" on hand, including sodium, calcium, potassium, and magnesium (the minerals best suited to neutralize acids). Maintaining these vital reserves—or better yet, boosting them—stops the development of pathogens and helps expel toxins, reducing stress on tissues and organs. The result is mineral-rich blood; increased physical strength, stamina, and

how to test your pH

There are a couple of ways to monitor your overall pH: live-blood analysis performed by a trained practitioner or a home test of your saliva or urine. Paper pH test strips are available online and from most pharmacies. The pH of saliva (tested by placing the strip on your tongue) tends to vary and is not as accurate as urine testing. For this, test the first of the day by dipping the strip into a sample of urine, or peeing directly onto the strip. (You only need a couple of drops from the first stream.) The optimal result is around 7.2. If your result is below 7.0 you can quickly rebalance your system by eating alkaline foods like cucumber, avocado, or asparagus, or drinking a six-ounce glass of water mixed with mineral salts (see page 208 for alkaline resources).

energy; improved mental clarity; and greater ability to combat disease and infection. In the bargain, alkaline buffers promote healthy skin, nails, and hair. It's a win-win.

---

note: It is common to be confused by the fact that some foods, such as lemons and limes, are acidic by nature but become alkaline-forming in our bodies.

Neutralizing a single acid particle takes about twenty alkaline particles. With numbers like that, we need all the alkaline help we can get. A healthy alkaline body is best supported by a healthy alkaline lifestyle. This starts with food choices. Keep stocked up on alkaline fuel: mineral-rich leafy and non-starchy vegetables; low-sugar fruits like lemon, lime, and grapefruit; avocado; coconut; sprouted nuts and seeds; cold-pressed fats and oils; mineral salts; and alkaline water. These foods provide electrical energy to the body, boost our alkaline buffer warriors, and starve the nasties that make us sick.

High-chlorophyll foods like leafy greens, rich in calcium and iron, help to improve the alkaline quality of the blood and boost the oxygenation of red blood cells. The more oxygen in the body, the less acid is produced.

Exercise—walking, rebounding (jumping on a mini trampoline), deep breathing, stretching, and yoga—also help support alkalinity by pumping the lymphatic system to eliminate acids and toxins. And, because stress is acidic, maintaining a positive attitude has a real benefit.

Here are some of the alkaline stars.

chlorophyll-rich foods

This is a category of pretty perfect foods that includes leafy greens (spinach and kale), sea vegetables, green leafy sprouts, cereal grasses (wheat, oat, and barley), herbs like parsley and cilantro, green beans, asparagus, and celery. Loaded with vitamins, minerals, fiber, antioxidants, and antifungal and antimicrobial agents, these vegetables provide oxygen that beneficial bacteria *love*. They're also detoxifying, regenerating, and hydrating to boot! A high-chlorophyll diet helps our blood cells deliver oxygen. In fact, chlorophyll is so close in molecular structure to the hemoglobin in our red blood cells that doctors used it for transfusions during World War II when facing shortages of blood plasma.

I supplement my consumption of chlorophyll-rich vegetables by drinking diluted liquid chlorophyll throughout the day. Start with 1 tablespoon in a 16-ounce (240ml) glass of water and build up. I do not use products containing chlorophyllin,

the semi-synthetic sodium/copper derivative of chlorophyll, which is cheaper but less effective, and of questionable quality. I do add concentrated green powders (containing a mixture of the chlorophyll-rich foods listed earlier) to water and to smoothies (see page 63).

Green vegetables balance acidity, digest quickly using very little energy, and contain valuable live enzymes, vitamins, and minerals. Their juices strengthen bodily functions, keeping organs, glands, and cells cleansed. Savory, low-sugar juices and smoothies are excellent at bolstering immunity. High-sugar juices and smoothies, on the other hand, promote acidity. I consume them in moderation for fun. To counteract their acidic effects, add in some apple cider vinegar, lemon juice, mineral salt, or probiotic powder, depending on what fits the flavor profile.

avocados

Among the world's most perfect foods, avocados are rich in vitamins, minerals, and highly digestible fats and proteins. They also contain the magical antioxidant nutrient glutathione, which repairs cell and tissue damage, calms inflammation, clears the respiratory tract, and regulates metabolism. I include a few avocados every day in smoothies, salads, wraps, and other dishes.

tomatoes

Tomatoes are powerfully alkalizing when raw and only mildly acidic when cooked. Combining tomatoes with avocados heightens the bioavailability of their nutrients. A salad of chopped avocado, tomato, olive oil, lemon juice, and salt makes for a mineral-rich, alkalizing pick-me-up or meal.

lemons, limes, and grapefruits

These citrus are chemically acidic but alkalize the body when metabolized, thanks to their high concentration of mineral salts. Squeezing their juices onto food or into drinking water, or adding the juice and flesh to smoothies, salads, soups, and other dishes is extremely beneficial.

cucumbers

One of my go-to foods, it is high in alkalizing minerals, mild in flavor, low in calories, incredibly versatile, and one of the most hydrating foods on the planet. I add it to smoothies and juices to balance sugars, throw it in salads, and devour it with dips and spreads.

live sprouts

Rich in vitamins, minerals, and complete proteins, live sprouts are magical foods—they transfer their alkaline life energy right into our bodies. They also bring greater diversity to our diets, since we can sprout grains and nuts, not just beans and seeds (see page 23).

healthy fats and oils

Our bodies need the essential fatty acids omegas 3, 6, and 9. Those contained in cold-pressed oils (coconut, avocado, hemp, flax, grapeseed, and olive), raw nuts and seeds, olives, fruits, and vegetables strengthen cells, lubricate joints, insulate the body, bind and eliminate acids, and provide energy. These plant-based sources are all naturally alkaline, and I seize every opportunity to include them in my diet.

water

Water is crucial for all bodily functions and for neutralizing and expelling acids through the sweat glands, bladder, and bowels. Our bodies are about 70 percent water, and just existing dehydrates us! Adults lose, on average, three liters of fluid each day just by breathing, sleeping, moving, sweating, and urinating. Constant replenishment by eating as many high-water-content foods as possible (leafy greens, vegetables, and low-sugar fruits) and consuming at least eight to ten glasses of water daily is key.

The best water is oxygenated, electron-rich, purified alkaline water. An ionizing machine that you attach to your faucet is a wise (albeit pricey) investment. Using a portable jug with an alkalizing filter is an inexpensive alternative (see box, above).

filtered water

I use filtered water because it tastes better, works better, and is better for us. You can spend as much on a filter and ionizing system as on your car or you can use an inexpensive portable jug with a replaceable filter. Water quality varies greatly with location and so does the question of adequate filtration. My recipes will, of course, work with tap water, but your body will be doing the filtering.

Whatever water you're drinking, you can alkalize it by adding pH drops. These drops (containing sodium/potassium bicarbonate, sodium chloride, and/or sodium chlorite) can be purchased at health food stores and online. Note that the drops increase the pH, but do not filter or cleanse the water.

note: Distilled water does aid with detoxification, but it has been de-ionized and contains no minerals, so is not good for everyday drinking.

salt

To survive, our bodies need salt in addition to water and oxygen. Adults have about a pound of salt, and all of our bodily fluids are saline. Mineral salts (containing sodium bicarbonate, potassium bicarbonate, magnesium chloride, and calcium chloride) strengthen the blood. Their electrolytes conduct electricity throughout the body, helping to maintain alkaline pH and alkaline buffers.

Given how insistently we're told that salt is horrible for us, this may sound nuts. It's true that ordinary table salt (highly processed, chemically cleaned, bleached, and stripped of its minerals) is, indeed, detrimental. It often contains additives, preservatives, fluoride, dextrose, aluminum hydroxide, and anti-caking agents that require a tremendous amount of energy to metabolize and get rid of. Natural, unrefined, mineral-rich salts, however, are a different story.

High-quality sea salt and Himalayan crystal salt are great options. Even better are the compound mineral salts mentioned above. These salts all alkalize the body and help to regulate the digestive, circulatory, and lymphatic systems. You can dilute these salts in water and drink them. If you can't find them (and they can be pricey), drinking 1 teaspoon of sodium bicarbonate (baking soda) in a 16-ounce (240ml) glass of water several times a day is also effective. Alternatively, there are natural liquid colloidal mineral salts (containing sodium and potassium bicarbonate) that can be sprayed on foods or directly into your mouth.

With all due respect for the Grateful Dead, acid is the enemy. It weakens our bodies. Parasites, yeasts, fungi, bacteria, viruses, and cancer cells just *love*

salt

I use Celtic sea salt or Himalayan crystal salt, which are harvested and sold as they come from the ocean or the earth. Rich in alkalizing minerals, they help provide energy, replenish electrolytes, fight bacterial infection, and aid digestion. These salts taste better than common table salt and they enhance flavors, particularly those of fruits and vegetables. The salt quantities in the recipes are calculated using high-quality varieties. If using regular table salt (processed, and generally containing additives), you'll want to start with half the amount and season to taste.

an acidic environment so they can poison our pancreas and liver, exhaust our adrenal and thyroid glands, and gobble up our energy reserves.

When our alkaline minerals are depleted, the body starts leaching them from the blood, bones, cartilage, and muscles. This starts a vicious cycle of chronic acidity. The blood dumps excess acid into tissues, then the lymphatic system neutralizes what it can, becomes overloaded, and dumps the acid back into the blood. This strains the liver, kidneys, and connective tissue. The circulatory system can't cope, and deposits excess acid as tumors, polyps, cysts, and other growths in the heart, liver, pancreas, and colon. It also gets stored in fatty tissue in the breasts, hips, thighs, belly, and brain. Chronic acidosis literally *corrodes* our bodies, leading to chronic inflammation, mineral deficiency, and the proliferation of disease. I feel sick just thinking about it.

• • •

Maybe you're frantically reaching for the baking soda, natural salt, and lemons; considering hocking your prized possessions for an alkaline water machine; and simultaneously contemplating overdosing on raw, sprouted, and probiotic-rich foods, while swearing off sugar and all manner of foods that aren't properly combined for the rest of your life. But the moral of the story is balance. And eat your greens.

Now, grab your blender, and let's have some fun!

natural sweeteners

Choose natural sweeteners to fit the personality of your blend. If texture's a concern, use a liquid sweetener. Combining sweeteners can yield great results. With substitutions, it's best to swap a liquid for a liquid, granular for granular, and powder for powder.

Stevia, a natural, calorie- and sucrose-free herb, does not alter blood-sugar levels, making it a fantastic alkaline sugar alternative. Antifungal and anti-inflammatory, stevia is a powerful supplement for regulating bodily function and increasing energy. Available as crushed leaves, powdered, or in liquid form, stevia is heat stable and ideal for use in cooked *and* raw recipes. (I call for alcohol-free stevia in the raw and alkaline recipes. Stevia with alcohol isn't raw.) I prefer the liquid because you can measure it drop by drop. My brand is Sweet Leaf, which also offers flavored alcohol-free liquid stevias—chocolate, vanilla, toffee, and others. Nu Naturals is a good producer, too; I use its lemon and orange flavors.

With stevia powder, it's easy to oversweeten. To make your own liquid, mix together 1 teaspoon of powder and 3 tablespoons of water. A teaspoon of this solution has the sweetening power of about 1 cup (200g) of sugar. Pure stevia is potent, and about 300 times sweeter than sugar. In large amounts, it has a bitter aftertaste. I add a small amount of stevia to alkaline juices, smoothies, and healing tonics, and to desserts in conjunction with other sweeteners and pronounced flavors. Read the labels—many stevia products contain fillers.

Maple syrup adds a delicious smoky flavor and is widely available and friendly to conventional blenders. It likes to be the star, so use small amounts and work your way up.

Coconut nectar and **raw agave nectar** can be substituted for other sweeteners in many recipes. The sugar profile of agave is problematic, so I use it in small amounts—where mild flavor or pale color is preferable.

Crude, unsulfured **blackstrap molasses** is rich in iron, calcium, and magnesium and is the only form of sugar that is alkaline forming. Molasses has a forceful personality, so I use it in small amounts blended with other sweeteners, like **brown rice syrup**, which is quite mild.

Yacon syrup is excellent, but not cheap or easy to find.

Pitted **dates** support base flavors beautifully, and I use them a lot. Always soak them, as they can be difficult to incorporate.

My pick in granulated sweeteners is **coconut sugar**, which has a low glycemic index and a rich flavor, and tends to give blends a caramel-like color.

For a caramel flavor, **lucuma powder** is a great raw option. But like yacon syrup, lucuma is expensive and not widely stocked by retailers.

Fruit and fruit juices—apple, pear, orange, grape, and pineapple—give a diversity of flavor options. A splash is often all it takes. Applesauce and other pure-fruit spreads are great, too.

Carrot juice has a surprising sweetness, as do **nut butters** and **coconut meat**. They all help to take the edge off the bitter aftertaste of stevia in alkaline blends.

Rose water, another top tip, adds natural decadence.

the recipes

smoothies & shakes

This decadent dessert shake tastes just like a melted cheesecake and will satisfy even the most in-withdrawal cream dreamer. But to get the full effect, you gotta soak those nuts! I created a similar smoothie for Driscoll's berries for their Vitamix sweepstakes, and when it was announced in the weekly newsletter, their website got so many hits, it crashed. 'Nuff said. Tart up and turn lemons into raspberry-lemon cheesecake.

raspberry-lemon cheesecake

SERVES 2, but you might not feel like sharing

1 cup (240ml) coconut water or water

1/2 teaspoon probiotic powder (optional; see note, page 30)

3/4 cup (105g) raw unsalted cashews, soaked (see page 22)

1 cup (160g) raspberries, fresh or frozen

1/2 banana

3 tablespoons freshly squeezed lemon juice, plus more to taste

1 tablespoon pure maple syrup, plus more to taste

1 teaspoon alcohol-free vanilla extract

1 pinch finely grated lemon zest, plus more to taste

Pinch of natural salt (optional, to boost flavors; see box, page 38)

1 cup (125g) ice cubes (more if using fresh berries)

Throw all of the ingredients into your blender and blast on high for about 1 minute, until smooth and creamy. Tweak flavors to taste (you may like a bit more lemon juice, sweetener, or zest).

SunCafe, my favorite local raw restaurant, won SeriousEats.com's Best Smoothie in L.A. award for a blend that's similar to this one. I'm not sure exactly what they put in their award-winner, but this is pretty close. One taste and you'll understand why kale-phobic omnivores line up and even double-park in front of SunCafe to run in and get their fill. Still the most popular recipe on my website, this is the Holy Grail of Kale.

tastes-like-ice-cream kale

SERVES 2

1/2 cup (120ml) water

1/2 teaspoon probiotic powder (optional; see note, page 30)

1/2 cup (70g) raw unsalted cashews, soaked (see page 22)

1 cup (25g) torn-up curly green kale leaves (1 or 2 large leaves with stalk removed, ripped into small pieces), plus more to taste

2 ripe bananas, fresh or frozen

1/4 cup (43g) chopped pitted dates, soaked (see page 22), or 1 tablespoon pure maple syrup, plus more to taste

1/2 teaspoon alcohol-free vanilla extract

2 cups (250g) ice cubes (a little less if using frozen bananas)

1/2 teaspoon minced ginger, plus more to taste (optional)

Put all of the ingredients into your blender in the order listed and puree for about a minute, until smooth and creamy. Tweak flavors to taste (you may like a bit more kale, sweetener, or ginger).

note: With a conventional blender, you'll get the smoothest consistency if you use maple syrup or chop the dates finely.

One of my all-time favorite green smoothies, this packs a powerful punch without pushing out the paunch. It bursts with complex flavors that dance on the tip of your tongue and tickle your throat long after they've massaged your belly. This one is a stunner, and it does justice to every bite of even the best pineapple salsa. It's not to be missed.

pineapple salsa

SERVES 2

1 cup (240ml) coconut water or water

2¹/₂ cups (400g) diced pineapple, fresh or frozen

1 cup (43g) firmly packed baby spinach

1¹/₂ teaspoons finely chopped red onion, plus more to taste

2 tablespoons chopped cucumber

¹/₄ cup (7g) finely chopped cilantro

1 teaspoon finely chopped jalapeño chile, plus more to taste

2 tablespoons freshly squeezed lime juice, plus more to taste

Pinch of finely grated lime zest

Pinch of natural salt, plus more to taste (optional, to bring out flavors; see page 38)

1 cup (125g) ice cubes (none if using frozen pineapple)

Natural sweetener (optional; see page 39)

Put all of the ingredients into your blender in the order listed and puree for about 1 minute, until smooth and creamy. Tweak flavors to taste (you may want more onion, jalapeño, lime juice, salt, or sweetener, depending on the ripeness of your pineapple; I find I never need it, but different strokes . . .).

This incredible savory blend of vegetables could easily be enjoyed as a cold soup. Complex and satisfying, the flavors explode up front, expand in the mouth, and keep partying in your throat until the next sip hits your lips. Make a meal out of this one.

spicy gazpacho grab

SERVES 2

4 tomatoes, quartered

$1/2$ red bell pepper, quartered and seeded

$1/2$ cucumber, peeled and roughly chopped

$1/2$ avocado, pitted and peeled

1 tablespoon finely chopped red onion, plus more to taste

2 tablespoons finely chopped cilantro

2 tablespoons freshly squeezed lime juice, plus more to taste

$1/2$ teaspoon natural salt, plus more to taste (see box, page 38)

$1/8$ teaspoon freshly ground black pepper

Pinch of red pepper flakes (optional, but really good)

1 cup (125g) ice cubes

Throw the tomatoes into your blender, then pile on the rest of the ingredients. Blast on high speed for 30 to 60 seconds, until smooth and creamy. Tweak flavors to taste (you may want more onion, lime juice, or salt).

This blendsation tastes like ice cream and is a protein powerhouse containing spinach, almond butter, and hemp seeds. Pears pair beautifully with the earthiness of the other ingredients, and ginger wakes up the party. If your pears are really sweet, you could leave out the date. Note that the ginger mellows as the smoothie sits. So, if you're not a fan of its flavor, let the blend chill in the fridge for a half hour.

perfect protein power

SERVES 2

1 cup (240ml) unsweetened almond or hemp milk (strained if homemade)

1/2 teaspoon probiotic powder (optional; see note, page 30)

1 tablespoon vegan vanilla protein powder (hemp, rice, or other)

3 ripe pears, skin on, cored and diced

2 cups (86g) firmly packed baby spinach

1/2 banana

2 tablespoons raw almond butter (not peanut butter; it's overpowering)

1 tablespoon freshly squeezed lime juice, plus more to taste

2 teaspoons minced fresh ginger

1 teaspoon shelled hemp seeds

Pinch of natural salt (see box, page 38)

1 cup (125g) ice cubes

1 date, pitted and soaked (see page 22)

Throw everything into your blender and blast on high speed for 30 to 60 seconds, until smooth and creamy. Tweak lime juice to taste.

protein powders

The easiest way to incorporate protein powder into your routine is to blend it into a smoothie. Look for products composed of organic, raw, sprouted ingredients and made without additives, preservatives, or sweeteners. I find that with all protein powders, as regards flavor and texture, less is more. I start with 1 teaspoon and add gradually. My go-to: plain hemp protein.

maqui berries

Maqui berries deliver the highest load of antioxidants among all fruits that have been measured. Maqui powder, still a niche ingredient, is typically available online and at select health food stores. The powder has a very mild flavor and does not alter the taste of this blend, so simply omit it if you don't have it. Açaí powder, on the other hand, is widely available, but feel free to omit it as well if you don't have any.

I think of this powerful blend as "field to shield." With the antioxidant weight of these ingredients, nothin's gettin' the better of you! You can enjoy this booster in summer with a little sweetener and omit the trio of orange zest, cinnamon, and ginger. But, these warming spices taste absolutely incredible with the berries, really pull the other flavors together, and elevate this smoothie from good to great. The açaí and maqui are optional but provide an invaluable boost, and I always include them. If you don't add these superfoods or the spices, you may not need the dates. However you make it, this one's got your back.

antioxidant avenger

SERVES 2

1/2 cup (120ml) coconut water

1/2 teaspoon probiotic powder (optional; see note, page 30)

1 packet (3.5 ounces/100g) frozen açaí pulp, or 2 table-spoons dried açaí powder (optional; see note, opposite page)

2 teaspoons maqui powder (optional; see note, opposite page)

2 cups (320g) mixed fresh or frozen berries (1/2 cup each of blueberries, blackberries, raspberries, and strawberries)

1/2 cup (85g) red seedless grapes

1 ripe pear, skin on, cored and diced

1/2 teaspoon minced ginger (optional)

1/4 teaspoon ground cinnamon (optional)

1/2 teaspoon finely grated orange zest (optional)

1 cup (125g) ice cubes

1 chopped pitted date, soaked, plus more to taste (optional; see box, page 22)

Throw everything into your blender and puree on high for 30 to 60 seconds, until smooth and creamy. Tweak the sweetness to taste.

slick smoothies

Whether you're making a nutrient-dense meal, a protein-packed workout booster, or a sweet treat, the flavor combinations possible in smoothies are endless, and you can tweak them right up to the moment of serving. There's rarely a "point of no return," so it's possible to rescue a seemingly undrinkable concoction by adding a piece of fruit, a bit of juice or zest, some chocolate, spices, herbs, or a sweetener. This forgiving quality of smoothies makes them a fabulous way for children and novice cooks to get creative and gain confidence in the kitchen.

When I make a smoothie, I choose ingredients for nutrition *and* pleasure in equal measure. A basic smoothie has three essential elements.

- Liquid—water, coconut water, juice, milk, kefir, kombucha, tea
- Base Ingredients—fruits, vegetables, nuts, seeds, powdered supplements
- Chill Factor—frozen fruits and vegetables, ice, flavored ice, cold liquid

These components alone inspire all kinds of wonderful-tasting blends. But to amp up the wow factor and keep things interesting, I have a few key strategies for creating spectacular smoothies.

The smoothie recipes in this chapter illustrate how I implement the ideas presented in this section, and they range from requiring a few ingredients and a few minutes of prep time, to a dozen ingredients and up to fifteen minutes hands-on. The latter may seem a bit full-on for a drink, but I approach these more-involved smoothies as meals, and sip them over the course of a half hour at least. (As digestion begins in the mouth, blend-and-gulp isn't the best approach.) If you use your blender for nothing more than a smoothie a day, you're getting your money's worth. Use the following tips to create your own combinations and make some s'blended discoveries.

mix it up

Use a wide range of fruits and vegetables for flavor, texture, color, and nutritional diversity. Freeze, stew, or dry produce that has been picked at the peak of ripeness and flavor for use all-year-round. Unsweetened purees like pear and apricot, as well as pumpkin butter and applesauce are great flavor boosters.

Don't rule out fresh, frozen, roasted, or steamed vegetables. Our taste buds are temperature sensitive and veggies are a lot milder when they're frozen. (In small quantities, you won't even taste them.) My favorite fresh vegetables are leafy greens, carrots, onions, peas, and fruits that we use like vegetables, such as cucumbers, tomatoes, and avocados. My frozen picks are cauliflower, broccoli, peas, brussels sprouts, spinach, and carrots. Cooked options include sweet potato, pumpkin, squash, carrots, beets, and cauliflower.

veggies first

Sweet fruits can transform even the most tragic of smoothies, but to prevent sugar spikes, I recommend a moderate intake of fruit drinks, balanced with vegetable blends containing a lot of leafy greens and a small amount of apple and lemon. These savory alkaline smoothies contain complex carbohydrates that are more slowly absorbed and metabolized than the sugars in fruits. Served chilled, they can expand your repertoire of cold soups. You can also simply tone down the sugar rush in fruit smoothies by adding a few handfuls of mild-tasting greens like spinach or romaine. They boost goodness while barely changing flavor. Adding a splash of apple cider vinegar or a bit of natural salt balances acidic blends, too.

milk to silk

Rich and creamy is the way I roll. Homemade milks (see page 28), kefir, kombucha, tea, and carrot juice make it into sweet blends, and coconut water, plain water, or vegetable juice are my go-to staples for savory blends. Yogurt and ice cream, too, achieve sensational results, but I rarely use them, to limit sugars and other additives.

juicing versus blending

Which is better, juicing or blending? This is a lively debate, but I prefer not to weigh in. There's a place for both in any healthy lifestyle. I blend every day and juice every week. I also do a weekly juice fast/cleanse, and for three days at the beginning of every season to empty and strengthen my system. During a cleanse or when I'm ill, I drink juices, both pulped and pulp-free, as they accommodate gentler digestion, leaving more energy for detoxification and regeneration. At all other times, I blend smoothies to retain the healthy fiber and nutrients in skins, piths, and even seeds. Smoothies are preferable to juices for everyday consumption, as the fiber they contain slows down the assimilation of sugars, assists with bowel regularity, and helps eliminate toxins.

i dream of creamy

For a smooth-textured and flavor-rich finish, throw in some avocado, coconut meat, or creamed coconut, or raw cashews, macadamias, or almonds. A tablespoon of tahini, or almond, cashew, hazelnut, macadamia, pecan, or sunflower seed butter adds a decadent flavor and texture. Banana is fabulous but has a dominant flavor and high sugar content. Other naturally creamy fruits like mango, pineapple, and nectarine are preferable, but still bring in a lot of natural sugar. Cooked carrot, sweet potato, squash, pumpkin, and cauliflower are great alternatives. Cooked or soaked raw grains can be effective. A little does it, unless you want your smoothie to taste like day-old porridge. Organic, non-GMO sprouted silken tofu works well, too, but due to its phytoestrogens (which can interfere with the body's normal hormonal balance), I consume soy in moderation.

flavor, sweet, and heat

A little sweetener can lift bland ingredients, take the edge off extreme flavors, and balance a blend. I typically use stevia (see page 39). However, for many people, stevia's aftertaste (reminiscent of artificial sweeteners) disqualifies it in favor of natural sugars. I like pitted dates, coconut sugar, coconut nectar, maple syrup, maple sugar, yacon syrup, and lucuma powder.

Ginger, cinnamon, nutmeg, cardamom, turmeric, chile, paprika, cayenne, and other spices give smoothies a kick, stimulate the lymph, and help detoxify the body. Fresh herbs like cilantro, mint, basil, parsley, dill, and chives add sensational flavor. Garlic offers a boost to savory blends, pairs surprisingly well with some fruits, and acts as an immune booster. Natural extracts, such as vanilla, almond, lemon, orange, hazelnut, and peppermint, are great accent flavors, and a nip of orange blossom/flower water or rose water adds an exotic twist. Then there's cacao, unsweetened cocoa, carob powder, and naturally flavored protein powder.

surely you zest

The juice and zest of lemon and lime brighten flavors and give flat smoothies a refreshing lift and zing. They're also powerful alkalizers (see page 37). I often add a whole peeled lime or some lemon juice to green smoothies. Orange zest is delicious but likes to be the star, so use it with a light hand. Alternatively, apples (which are less assertive than citrus) add flavor and mask the taste of pungent or earthy vegetables.

nuts and seeds, protein powders, superfoods

Raw cashews, macadamias, and pecans bring a rich, creamy, buttery texture and decadent taste to smoothies. Other nuts, such as Brazil nuts, almonds, and walnuts, and seeds like chia, sacha inchi, flax, hemp, pumpkin, sesame, and sunflower, boost the health profile of blends. Activate the nutrient potential of nuts and seeds by soaking (see page 21).

For natural protein powder, hemp is a favorite. But mix things up for flavor diversity and nutrient joy. Look for products that include high-quality, raw, sprouted ingredients. Texture is important, too, as many brands are gritty. (See Resources, page 209.) Heavy additions of protein powder can leave a powdery aftertaste, compromising the balance of other ingredients. Start with a small amount and add to taste.

With nutrient-dense superfoods you only need a teaspoon or a tablespoon, making them a cost-effective smoothie enhancment. I enjoy adding flax, chia, or hemp seeds; lucuma, maca, mesquite, or açai powder; wheatgrass; berries like goji, camu, maqui, and mulberries; and green algaes like spirulina and chlorella. (See Resources, page 209.)

clean and green makes you gleam

Blending green veggies into a smoothie is a great way to increase your vegetable consumption. These chlorophyll-rich goodies help to alkalize the system; combat disease and infection; and promote healthy skin, nails, and hair. Ease into the green smoothie experience. Start with fruit-based blends using some coconut water, plain water, or milk and small amounts of leafy greens with flavors that are easily masked, such as spinach, romaine,

---

Alkaloids in some leafy green vegetables (such as oxalic acid in spinach) can inhibit absorption of minerals like calcium and iron. To avoid this, simply rotate your greens daily and blend a variety. Rotation expands nutritional range as well as taste-bud satisfaction.

---

and mustard. Once your taste buds have acclimated to the green additions, reduce the fruit and increase the vegetables. From gateway greens, move on to the strong stuff: kale and chard; collard, beet, carrot, and turnip greens; and parsley, cilantro, mint, and basil. Finally, advance to wild edibles: grasses, dandelion greens, pigweed, lamb's quarter, broadleaf plantain, hibiscus, nasturtiums, and other forage. The flavor dimensions of green smoothies go way beyond those of fruits.

oil your engine

Flaxseed, hemp, borage, avocado, coconut, macadamia, pumpkin seed, and olive oil are healthy smoothie additions. With oil, start small. A little goes a long way; too much can completely change the personality of your blend. Assemble the liquid and base of your smoothie first, blend, and add just a teaspoon or two of oil to taste (or so that you can't taste it).

flavored ice is *nice*!

Approximate the magic of ice cream or sorbet in a healthy smoothie by using flavored ice. Pour fruit or vegetable juice, nut milk, or tea into ice cube trays, freeze, and you're set. My favorites: coconut, almond, and cashew milk; pineapple, apple, carrot, and spinach juice; herbal teas like chamomile and peppermint; green tea; and fresh herbs like basil and mint frozen in water. Just note that flavored ices (especially those with a high fat and sugar content) are softer than regular ice and will melt more quickly.

gloat, don't bloat

Some people experience bloating after drinking smoothies. In many cases, this can be avoided by paying attention to food combining (see page 31). For some, combining fruits and vegetables wreaks digestive havoc, for others it doesn't. Find what works for you. Leafy greens generally combine well with all foods. However, there are exceptions. If you're feeling bloated, avoid combining nut milk, nuts, seeds, and grains with fruits, and try soaking your nuts and seeds (see page 21).

seal the deal

Consuming smoothies immediately after making them minimizes oxidation and degradation of nutrients. To store a smoothie to drink within a few hours, transfer the blend to a glass jar, seal, and chill. For consumption within twenty-four hours, encase the jar in a vacuum-sealed pouch and squeeze out the air. Freezing smoothies is not ideal, but it's better than going without. Fill an airtight container three-quarters full (to allow for expansion of the liquid as it freezes), freeze for no more than 2 to 3 weeks, thaw partway, and re-blend to revive the prize!

build your own smoothie

Choose one or two items from each category and find your perfect blend.

Liquid (1 to 2 cups)	Cream	Greens (1 to 2 cups)	Boost	Magic (to taste)
Water or coconut water	1 avocado, banana, or mango	Alfalfa, chard, kale, mache, romaine, spinach	1 tablespoon acai or wheatgrass	**Spices:** cinnamon, ginger, cayenne, nutmeg, cardamom, turmeric, or chile
Coconut, almond, or hemp milk	1 cup raw coconut meat	Beet, collard, dandelion, or mustard greens	1 tablespoon chia seeds, hemp seeds, or flax seeds	**Herbs:** mint, basil, cilantro, or parsley
Kefir or kombucha	1/4 cup cooked grains or silken tofu		1 tablespoon goji berries, maqui berries, or mulberries	**Zest:** lemon, lime, or orange
Herbal or green tea	Handful of raw cashews, macadamias, blanched almonds, or hemp seeds	Broccoli, pea, or radish sprouts	1 teaspoon maca or mesquite	**Natural extracts:** vanilla, almond, peppermint, rose water, or orange blossom water
Base (2 or 3 servings)	1 to 2 tablespoons nut butter	Cilantro, mint, or parsley	1/4 teaspoon spirulina or chlorella	**Sweetener:** stevia, dates, maple syrup, coconut sugar, coconut nectar, lucuma powder, yacon syrup, or brown rice syrup
Fruits or vegetables (dried, fresh, frozen, or cooked)	1/2 cup yogurt or milk ice cubes		1 scoop hemp protein powder or other blend	
Raw nuts and seeds			1 tablespoon coconut, hemp, flax, avocado, macadamia, or olive oil	

Be open-minded with this one (see photo, page 58). It sounds disgusting but is surprisingly delicious. Packed with anti-inflammatory power (a virtue of the spices in yellow curry), this is a fabulous warming smoothie for cold months. In hot weather, omit the curry powder and pepper flakes and you've got a delicious tropical-fruit smoothie that will appeal to just about anybody. Two for the price of one. You gotta love that.

tropical fruit curry

SERVES 2

2 cups (480ml) water

1/2 cup (120ml) canned coconut milk (shake, then pour)

1 cup (160g) diced mango, fresh or frozen

1 cup (160g) diced pineapple, fresh or frozen

1 cup (160g) diced peaches, fresh or frozen

1/2 teaspoon finely grated lime zest, plus more to taste

2 cups (250g) ice cubes (if using fresh fruit)

1/2 teaspoon yellow curry powder

Pinch of red pepper flakes, plus more to taste

Pinch of natural salt (see box, page 38)

Natural sweetener (optional; see page 39)

Toss everything into your blender and blast on high for 30 to 60 seconds, until smooth and creamy. Tweak flavors to taste (you may want more lime zest, curry, pepper flakes, or sweetener).

Jam-packed with some of the top vitamin C fruits and vegetables, this smoothie (see photo, page 58) is bursting with goodness and flavor. The seemingly bizarre combination of fruit with cauliflower and sweet potato works in spectacular fashion to create a creamy and delicious blend, and is a tasty way to get kids to drink their vegetables. If you're concerned about the strong taste of the turmeric, start with $1/8$ teaspoon, which is usually undetectable. For a bigger boost of C, add some goji berries (soaked, if you're using a conventional blender) and flaxseeds. While this recipe appears a tad labor-intensive for a smoothie, it's actually quick to throw together if you have leftover sweet potato and all of your other ingredients organized. Load up!

creamy orange c

SERVES 2 TO 4

$1^1/_2$ cups (360ml) freshly squeezed orange juice

$1/_2$ teaspoon probiotic powder (optional; see note, page 30)

1 orange, peeled and seeded

1 cup (160g) roughly chopped strawberries

$1/_2$ cup (70g) diced red bell pepper

$1/_2$ cup (70g) roughly chopped baked or steamed orange sweet potato (peeled before or after cooking)

$1/_2$ cup (60g) frozen raw cauliflower florets

$1/_4$ cup (60g) firm silken tofu

$1/_4$ cup (35g) blanched, slivered raw almonds, soaked (see page 22)

2 teaspoons finely grated orange zest

1 teaspoon alcohol-free vanilla extract

$1/_8$ teaspoon ground turmeric, plus more to taste

1 tablespoon pure maple syrup, or 5 drops alcohol-free liquid stevia, plus more to taste

2 cups (250g) ice cubes, plus more to taste

1 dried apricot, finely chopped (optional)

1 tablespoon dried goji berries (optional)

1 teaspoon ground flaxseeds (optional)

Throw everything into your blender and blast on high for 30 to 60 seconds, until smooth and creamy. Tweak flavors and consistency to taste (you may like a bit more turmeric, sweetener, or ice cubes) and enjoy.

From left: Papaya Pleasure,
Tropical Fruit Curry (page 56),
Creamy Orange C (page 57)

This tropical blend is a little earthy and woody, with delicate, simple flavors that are light and refreshing. Packed with foods that are good for your skin, it's a delicious morning rejuvenator.

papaya pleasure

SERVES 2

1 cup (240ml) unsweetened almond milk (strained if homemade)

2 cups (320g) roughly chopped papaya

3/4 cup (120g) roughly chopped fresh or frozen mango

2 teaspoons freshly squeezed lemon juice

2 teaspoons minced ginger, plus more to taste

1 teaspoon flaxseed oil

1/8 teaspoon ground cinnamon, plus more to taste

1/8 teaspoon finely grated lemon zest, plus more to taste

1/4 teaspoon alcohol-free vanilla extract

5 drops alcohol-free liquid stevia (see page 39), plus more to taste

1 cup (125g) ice cubes

Throw all of the ingredients into your blender and blast on high for about 1 minute, until smooth and creamy. Tweak flavors to taste (you may want more ginger, cinnamon, lemon zest, or sweetener).

vanilla

I break open a vanilla bean, spoon out vanilla paste, or use natural vanilla extract to enrich flavors. My recipes call for extract, as it's the most economical form, and specify natural (for cooked recipes) and alcohol-free (for raw and alkaline recipes). If using imitation vanilla or a vanilla-flavored product, reduce the quantity by half and tweak to taste.

This smoothie is a fun way to get kids to eat more veggies. Unlike the murky color of some vegetable smoothies, the brown of this smoothie makes it look like a chocolate milkshake, enabling you to hide all manner of nutritious goodies inside. And it's so delicious and creamy, nobody will know that it contains greens! Note that the broccoli must be frozen and the cauliflower must be steamed and cooled, not raw. This is quick and easy to make if you have a bit of leftover cauliflower. If you can't quite get your head around blending wet florets, you can always add an extra banana and reduce the sweetener.

chock-full chocolate surprise

SERVES 2 TO 4

1 cup (240ml) unsweetened soy, rice, hemp, or almond milk (strained if homemade)

1/2 teaspoon probiotic powder (optional; see note, page 30)

1/2 cup (22g) firmly packed baby spinach

1/4 cup (25g) frozen broccoli (about 2 florets)

1 banana, plus more to taste

1/2 ripe pear, cored, plus more to taste

1 cup (120g) steamed cauliflower florets (cooled completely), or an extra banana (to save time if you don't have a bit of leftover cauliflower)

2 tablespoons cacao powder or unsweetened cocoa powder, plus more to taste

2 teaspoons natural vanilla extract

2 tablespoons pure maple syrup, plus more to taste

1 cup (125g) ice cubes

Throw everything into your blender and puree on high for 30 to 60 seconds, until smooth and creamy. Tweak flavors to taste (you may like a bit more banana, pear, cacao, vanilla, or maple syrup).

note: This smoothie is best consumed immediately, or the day it is made.

Since this recipe was shared in a video I filmed with the team at Chow.com, I've been overwhelmed with emails of gratitude from happy apple pie devotees who are delighted that they can blend up their fix in less time than it takes to preheat the oven. Rich and creamy (if you soak the nuts), the cashews replicate the buttery flavor of pastry, making this joyfully reminiscent of that perfect bite à la mode. This blend rocks, and I don't mind sayin' so. Who eats humble pie anyway?

apple pie in a glass

SERVES 2

1 cup (240ml) unsweetened almond milk (strained if homemade)

1 cup (270g) unsweetened applesauce or stewed apples

1/2 teaspoon probiotic powder (optional; see note, page 30)

1/2 cup (70g) raw unsalted cashews, soaked (see page 22)

2 teaspoons natural vanilla extract, plus more to taste

1/2 teaspoon ground cinnamon, plus more to taste

2 chopped, pitted, and soaked (see page 22) dates, or 2 table-spoons pure maple syrup

1 cup (125g) ice cubes

Throw everything into your blender and blast on high for 30 to 60 seconds, until smooth and creamy. Tweak flavors to taste (you may want to add more vanilla, cinnamon, or sweetener).

note: Use the soaked dates with high-speed blenders and the maple syrup with conventional blenders.

I receive hundreds of emails a month asking the same question, "How do you make those disgusting green powders tolerable?" My answer is always the same, in all caps: MINT! And the right blend of cashews and banana, in the case of this blend. I almost left this recipe out of the book because I thought it might be a bit hard-core for anybody other than devoted green-smoothie drinkers. But my green-smoothie brigade begged me to include it. So, here it is. It's not for everyone, but it's the sexiest intro to green powders I've ever found.

minty green gluttony

SERVES 2

1 cup (240ml) unsweetened almond milk or hemp milk (strained if homemade)

1 cup (240ml) coconut water

1 tablespoon vanilla protein powder

1/2 teaspoon probiotic powder (optional; see note, page 30)

1 teaspoon wheatgrass powder (see note, below)

1/2 teaspoon spirulina powder (see note, below)

1/2 teaspoon chlorella powder (see note, below)

2 cups (86g) firmly packed baby spinach

2 cups (285g) frozen sliced banana (about 2 large)

3/4 cup (105g) raw unsalted cashews, soaked (see page 22)

1/4 cup (9g) firmly packed mint leaves

1 teaspoon alcohol-free vanilla extract

1/4 teaspoon peppermint extract, plus more to taste (optional)

1 tablespoon coconut nectar (see page 39) or 2 chopped, pitted, and soaked (see page 22) dates, plus more to taste

1 cup (125g) ice cubes, plus more to taste

Throw everything into your blender and blast on high for about 1 minute, until smooth and creamy. Tweak flavors and consistency to taste (you may like more peppermint, sweetener, or ice cubes).

note: You can substitute 2 teaspoons of an unsweetened green powder blend for the combined measures of wheatgrass, spirulina, and chlorella. Use the coconut nectar with conventional blenders and the soaked dates with high-speed blenders.

CHAPTER 4

appetizers, snacks, dips & spreads

This little treasure is one of those "maximum output for minimum input" recipes we all *luuuuv*. A seriously tasty tapenade (see photo, page 68), this crowd-pleaser gets blended up in minutes and makes you look like a rock star. Be sure to rinse your olives and capers to avoid an intensely salty experience. You don't have to make the crostini (gluten-free or otherwise), but my friend Chuck says a tapenade should always come with kick-ass crusty bread. And who am I to argue?

olive tapenade with crostini

MAKES 1³/₄ CUPS (400G) TAPENADE AND 2 TO 3 DOZEN CROSTINI

crostini

1 gluten-free baguette, sliced thin

1 to 2 tablespoons olive oil

1 clove garlic

Freshly ground black pepper (optional)

tapenade

¹/₄ cup (60ml) cold-pressed extra-virgin olive oil, plus more as needed

1 cup (130g) rinsed, pitted, and chopped kalamata olives

1 cup (120g) rinsed, pitted, and chopped green olives

2 teaspoons finely chopped garlic (about 2 cloves)

2 teaspoons capers, rinsed and drained

3 tablespoons chopped roasted red bell pepper (plain, from a jar is fine)

1 teaspoon freshly squeezed lemon juice, plus more to taste

2 tablespoons finely chopped flat-leaf parsley

Preheat the oven to 425°F (220°C).

Place your bread slices on a large baking sheet, drizzle with the olive oil, and then rub the garlic clove over the top of each slice. Bake for about 10 minutes, until just lightly browned. Remove from the oven and allow to cool.

As the crostini cools, pour the olive oil into the blender (or a food processor). Add the olives, garlic, capers, red bell pepper, and lemon juice. (If you're making the tapenade in a food processor, you can add the parsley as well.) Blast on high for just a few seconds. Pulse, adding more olive oil if needed, until everything is rustically combined. Stop the machine periodically and scrape down the sides of the container to incorporate everything. Taste and add more lemon juice if desired. Scoop the tapenade into a bowl, stir in the parsley, and serve with the crostini.

A healthier alternative to dairy-laden dips, this artichoke and white bean dip (see photo, page 71) is like hummus on steroids, and it tickles your taste buds with every bite. My friends love it with raw veggie sticks, pita chips, or flatbreads, or spread on wraps and sandwiches. The rosemary flavor intensifies if the dip stands or is chilled overnight, so if that herb's not a favorite, use half the amount called for. I've been known to devour it with Awesome Almond Crackers (page 70), directly out of the blender carriage. Yeah, I've got issues.

artichoke and white bean dip

MAKES 1 1/2 CUPS (400G)

1/4 cup (60ml) cold-pressed extra-virgin olive oil

1/4 cup (60ml) unsweetened almond or soy milk (strained if homemade)

1 (14-ounce/400g) can artichoke hearts, plain (not marinated), well rinsed and well drained

1 (15-ounce/425g) can cannellini beans, rinsed and drained

1 tablespoon plus 1 teaspoon freshly squeezed lemon juice

1 1/2 tablespoons diced yellow onion

1 1/2 teaspoons minced garlic (about 2 cloves)

3/4 teaspoon finely chopped rosemary (not dried)

1 teaspoon natural salt (see box, page 38)

1/2 teaspoon sweet paprika

1/8 teaspoon cayenne pepper

Throw everything into your blender and puree for about 1 minute, until smooth and creamy like hummus. (If you're using a conventional blender, you may need a tablespoon of water to help the blades do their work.) Transfer to a bowl, cover, and chill in the fridge until ready to serve.

From top: Olive Tapenade with Crostini (page 66), Incredibly Edible Edamame Dip

One of the enduring favorites on my website, this recipe is addictive. Not only because it tastes so darn good, but also because it only takes minutes to blend up and devour. However, the recipe only works in a high-speed blender or food processor. Use it as a dip with raw vegetables and crackers, or spread it on sandwiches or wraps. Totally guilt-free, super-healthy, alkalizing, and nutrient-dense, this one's a winner on all fronts.

incredibly edible edamame dip

MAKES 2 1/2 CUPS (550G)

3 tablespoons cold-pressed extra-virgin olive oil

2 cups (320g) shelled raw edamame beans

2 cups (54g) loosely packed baby spinach

1/4 cup (60ml) freshly squeezed lemon juice, plus more to taste

3 tablespoons tahini

1 1/2 tablespoons finely chopped onion (yellow, white, or Vidalia is good, but not red)

2 cloves garlic, minced, plus more to taste

1/4 teaspoon ground cumin

1/4 teaspoon red pepper flakes, plus more to taste

1 teaspoon natural salt (see box, page 38), plus more to taste

2 tablespoons sesame seeds (optional)

1/4 cup (12g) finely chopped flat-leaf parsley (optional)

Throw the oil, edamame, spinach, lemon juice, tahini, onion, garlic, cumin, pepper flakes, and salt into your high-speed blender or food processor and blend on high or process for about 2 minutes, until smooth and creamy. Stop the machine periodically and scrape down the sides of the container to fully incorporate the ingredients. A food processor will give the mixture a coarse consistency, which some people prefer. Tweak flavors to taste. (You may like more lemon juice, garlic, pepper flakes, or salt.) Serve topped with the sesame seeds and parsley.

These crackers are a fabulous alternative to the ubiquitous, fake-flavored cardboard-like slices so popular in snacking culture. They are just yum. Although these are devoid of preservatives, artificial flavors, and sugar, you could be forgiven for suspecting they contained some nasties. Getting their texture *juuust* right is a little tricky. Rolling the dough as thin as possible is key. My partner, Scott, devours these with my dairy-free butter (see page 202) and says they're better than his old processed favorites.

awesome almond crackers

MAKES 30 OR 29 OR 28 . . . depending on how many you scarf off the tray while they cool

1/4 cup (60ml) water

2 tablespoons olive oil

1 tablespoon freshly squeezed lemon juice

1 clove garlic, plus 1 more if you're a garlic lover

1/2 teaspoon granulated onion powder

1/2 teaspoon natural salt (see box, page 38)

1 1/2 cups (150g) blanched almond flour

1/4 cup (19g) ground flaxseeds

2 tablespoons shelled hemp seeds

1 tablespoon finely chopped rosemary

1 tablespoon finely chopped thyme

Preheat the oven to 300°F (150°C).

Throw the water, olive oil, lemon juice, garlic, onion powder, and salt into your blender. Blend just a few seconds, until the garlic is crushed and the liquids are combined. If you're using a conventional blender, slowly add the almond flour through the lid opening while the machine is running on low. If you're using a high-speed blender, just add the flour and blend on low until the dough thickens and comes together. Transfer the dough to a mixing bowl and stir in the ground flaxseeds, hemp seeds, and herbs.

Cut four large sheets of parchment paper to fit two large baking sheets. Divide the dough into two balls. Place one ball on a sheet of parchment paper. Place another piece of paper on top and using a rolling pin, gently roll out the dough. Get it as thin as possible, no more than 1/16 inch (1.5mm) thick. (Any thicker and the crackers won't get crispy.) Remove the top sheet of parchment paper and use a knife or pizza cutter to cut the dough into about 15 (2-inch/5cm) squares. Repeat with the second dough ball using the two remaining sheets of parchment. Place the parchment with the crackers on the baking sheets.

Bake for 8 to 10 minutes and then swap the baking sheets so the top one is on the bottom and vice versa. Bake for another 8 to 10 minutes, until the crackers are pale in the middle and just starting to brown on the edges. Remove from the oven and allow to cool on the baking sheets for about 30 minutes, until the crackers are crisp.

From top:
Artichoke and White Bean Dip (page 67),
Awesome Almond Crackers

say "cheeze"

Life is just better with a bit of cheeze. Here are three of my favorites. You need a dehydrator for the "parmesan" and "feta," but not for the basic variety. The miso paste, lemon juice, and apple cider vinegar combine to create a delicious tangy flavor, reminiscent of aged dairy cheeses. You can jazz up any of these cheezes with spices and fresh herbs. The sky's the limit.

basic creamy cheeze

MAKES ABOUT 2 CUPS (380G)

¹⁄₄ cup (60ml) plus 3 table-spoons unsweetened almond milk (strained if homemade), plus more as needed

2 tablespoons cold-pressed extra-virgin olive oil

3 tablespoons freshly squeezed lemon juice

1 cup (120g) blanched raw almonds, soaked (see page 22)

¹⁄₂ cup (70g) pine nuts, soaked (see page 22)

¹⁄₂ cup (70g) sunflower seeds, soaked (see page 22)

1 tablespoon white miso paste

1¹⁄₂ teaspoons wheat-free tamari

2 teaspoons minced garlic (about 2 cloves)

¹⁄₂ teaspoon natural salt (see box, page 38), plus more to taste

2 tablespoons finely chopped chives (optional)

2 tablespoons finely chopped flat-leaf parsley (optional)

Pour the milk, oil, and lemon juice into your blender and then add the nuts, seeds, miso paste, tamari, garlic, and salt. Puree on high for 1 to 2 minutes, until well combined and rustically creamy. You may have to stop the machine periodically and scrape down the sides of the container. You may also need to add a bit more milk to get the desired consistency. Scoop the cheeze into a bowl, stir in the herbs, and add more salt to taste. Place the bowl in the fridge for 1 hour to allow the cheeze to firm up a little before serving.

variation: Add some more garlic, some chile, and herbs of your choice, and this makes a wonderful dip!

pine nut "parmesan"

MAKES 1 1/2 CUPS (130G) FLAKES

3 tablespoons water, plus more as needed

3/4 teaspoon apple cider vinegar

2 tablespoons freshly squeezed lemon juice

1 cup (140g) raw pine nuts, soaked (see page 22)

1 1/2 tablespoons white miso paste

1 teaspoon natural salt (see box, page 38), plus more to taste

Throw all the ingredients into your blender in the order listed and blend for 1 to 2 minutes, until you have a smooth paste. Taste and add more salt to taste. If you're using a conventional blender, you may need to add another tablespoon or two of water to get the desired consistency. Line 3 dehydrator trays with nonstick sheets or parchment paper. Using a spatula, spread on the mixture in a very thin layer. Heat at 115°F (46°C) for about 8 hours, until the mixture is dry and firm on the top. Using a rubber spatula or your fingers, break up the cheeze into flakes. It should look like traditional parmesan. Toss the flakes and dry for another 1 to 2 hours, until they're hard and crumbly (the consistency of aged dairy cheese). Store in a sealed container in the fridge for up to a week, or in the freezer for up to 6 months.

macadamia "feta"

MAKES 1 1/2 CUPS (210G)

1/2 cup (120ml) unsweetened almond milk (strained if homemade)

1/4 cup (60ml) cold-pressed extra-virgin olive oil

3 tablespoons freshly squeezed lemon juice

1 teaspoon apple cider vinegar, plus more to taste

1 cup (135g) raw unsalted macadamias, soaked (see page 22)

2 tablespoons white miso paste

1 tablespoon finely chopped green onion (white and green parts)

1 1/2 teaspoons finely chopped garlic (about 2 cloves)

1 teaspoon natural salt (see box, page 38), plus more to taste

Throw all of the ingredients into your blender and blast on high for 1 to 2 minutes, until smooth and creamy. Your blender will start to labor as the mixture thickens. You may have to stop the machine periodically and scrape down the sides of the container. Tweak the flavors to get a tangy effect reminiscent of traditional feta (you may want more vinegar, lemon juice, or salt). Line 2 dehydrator trays with nonstick sheets or parchment paper. Use a 1/4-teaspoon measuring spoon to scoop clumps of the mixture onto the trays, like drop cookies in rows, and dehydrate at 115°F (46°C) for 8 to 12 hours, until dry on the outside but still tender on the inside. Store in an airtight container in the fridge for up to 5 days.

note: Blanched almonds work well in place of macadamias in this recipe.

fresh spring rolls with orange-almond sauce

MAKES 16 ROLLS

rolls

5.25 ounces (150g) vermicelli noodles, either mung bean and potato starch or rice

1/4 cup (60ml) wheat-free tamari or soy sauce

3 tablespoons coconut sugar (or other natural sweetener; see page 39)

4 large (7 ounces/200g) shiitake or cremini mushrooms, sliced

16 rice paper wrappers

8 large lettuce leaves, preferably soft ones, halved and hard ribs removed

2 large (or 4 small) green onions, white and green parts, julienned

1 large carrot, julienned

2 Persian or Lebanese cucumbers, julienned

1 cup (22g) loosely packed cilantro

1 cup (20g) loosely packed mint

1 cup (25g) loosely packed basil

1 large avocado, pitted, peeled, and sliced

dipping sauce

1/4 cup (60ml) water, plus more as needed

2 tablespoons plus 1/2 teaspoon freshly squeezed lime juice

2 tablespoons plus 1/2 teaspoon freshly squeezed orange juice

1/2 cup (120g) raw almond butter

1/2 teaspoon minced ginger

1 teaspoon coconut nectar (see page 39)

1/2 teaspoon finely chopped garlic (1/2 clove)

1/2 teaspoon wheat-free tamari or soy sauce

1/8 teaspoon red pepper flakes

Pinch of finely grated lime zest

To make the rolls, soak the noodles in hot water for about 20 minutes, until soft. In a sauté pan over high heat, bring the tamari and coconut sugar to a boil. Boil for about 1 minute, reduce the heat to medium-low, and simmer for 2 to 3 minutes, until thickened slightly. Throw in the mushrooms, increase the heat to medium, and bring the mixture to a gentle simmer. Cook for 15 minutes, stirring often, until the mushrooms are nice and caramelized. Remove the mushrooms from the pan and reserve the cooking liquid. It will only be a tablespoon or two. Drain the noodles completely and toss them with the reserved cooking liquid.

To assemble the rolls, fill a shallow dish half full with water and submerge one rice paper wrapper for 10 to 20 seconds, just long enough to soften. Remove the wrapper from the water and place on a work surface. Place a lettuce leaf in the middle of the wrapper and top it with a forkful of noodles, 2 or 3 pieces of mushroom, 2 green onion pieces, 4 sticks of carrot, 4 sticks of cucumber, 6 cilantro leaves, 4 mint leaves, 2 basil leaves, and 2 avocado slices. Fold the half of the wrapper closest to you up and over the filling, and then fold in the sides. Carefully roll up the spring roll and set it on a dish, seam-side down. Repeat with the remaining wrappers and filling. If not serving immediately, chill in the fridge, loosely covered, for up to 3 hours.

To make the dipping sauce, throw all of the ingredients into your blender and puree on high for about 1 minute, until well combined. You may want to add an additional tablespoon or two of water to thin out the sauce. Serve alongside the rolls.

I love Thai fresh rolls, and nobody I know makes them better than my friend Eda. Hers sell out in hours at the annual Lollapalooza music festival. I wasn't going to include a spring roll recipe without first running it by an expert. I also called in my friend and rolling ace, Nikki, and the results were spectacular. Eda's secret to making fabulous vegan spring rolls taste meaty is caramelized mushrooms, so I stole that brilliant trick for this recipe. "Oh, my!" Eda said of my orange-almond sauce, "Traditional, no. Delicious, yes!"

My friend Mika introduced me to this traditional delicacy enjoyed by Japanese monks, and I've been utterly addicted since my first euphoric taste. This chilled sensation is made with sesame (*goma*) instead of soy. I've served this to ardent tofu haters and they have begged on their knees for just one more bite. In Japanese monasteries, the junior monks grind the sesame seeds by hand so the older monks can get their fix. But who has time for that? I use a pure roasted, unsalted tahini or a plain sesame paste (just ground sesame seeds) from a Japanese grocer. This is then blended with kuzu-root powder and a seaweed broth called *kombu dashi* that is easy to make but requires an hour.

The sesame flavor is the star in this tofu, and sauces can overwhelm it, so plain old tamari and wasabi are my go-to accompaniments for ultimate pleasure. To cook the tofu, you must stir the mixture continuously with the patience of a monk because it can turn on a dime and burn. It takes some work, but is so worth it. I love it so much I may consider being reincarnated as a monk—but a senior one. I don't want to grind all those seeds!

gomadofu—chilled sesame tofu

SERVES 6 AS A STARTER, or if you're greedy like me, 4!

2 strips (8g) dried kombu

¹/₄ cup plus 2¹/₂ tablespoons (52g) finely ground kuzu-root powder (see Resources, page 208)

¹/₃ cup (60g) pure roasted, unsalted tahini or sesame paste, stirred very well

¹/₄ teaspoon natural salt (see box, page 38)

toppings

2 teaspoons wasabi powder mixed with 2 teaspoons water to form a paste

2 teaspoons wheat-free tamari, soy sauce, or Bragg liquid aminos (see page 132)

Clean (don't wash) the kombu with a damp cloth and immerse it in 3 cups (720ml) water. Let stand at room temperature for at least 1 hour. Remove the kombu and save to use in a salad or other dish. Make sure the kuzu-root powder is pulverized and stir it into 1 cup (240ml) of the kombu broth until thoroughly combined. Pour the mixture into your blender. Add the tahini, salt, and another 1¹/₂ cups (360ml) of kombu broth. Blend for about 30 seconds on medium, until smooth. Select your tofu mold. I use silicone ice cube trays for uniform chilling, easy unmolding, and beautiful presentation. A shallow, glass baking dish also works. Wet your mold with cold water to keep the tofu from sticking.

Pour the blend into a saucepan over medium-high heat. Stir continuously with a wooden spoon. After 1 or 2 minutes, the mixture will rapidly turn, thickening visibly. Reduce the heat to medium and continue to stir. Large bubbles will start to form. Keep stirring vigorously for 10 to 12 minutes, until the mixture has the texture of custard and coats the spoon thickly. Don't let the mixture stick to the bottom of the pan or burn.

Fill a large, shallow baking dish with very cold water and some ice cubes. Pour the mixture into your mold and smooth out the surface with a small spoon or spatula. It will start to set immediately, so work quickly. Place the molds into the ice water to set. (Don't place the mixture in the fridge or it will set too rapidly.) When the ice in the water bath melts, replace it. You may have to do this a second time. After about 40 minutes, the ice cubes will stop melting so rapidly. That's how you know it's ready. Once the *gomadofu* is completely set, cut it into squares (if you're using a large mold) or invert the ice cube tray on a plate and gently pop out the cubes.

To serve, set each square of tofu in a bowl topped with a tiny piece of wasabi paste and drizzle on ¼ teaspoon of tamari.

The French call these *socca*; the Italians call them *farinata*. These crispy thin pancakes or crepes are traditionally baked in a cast-iron skillet or tin-plated copper baking pan, in a wood-fire oven. But baking one big focaccia-style flatbread in a skillet or cake pan will get the best results in a conventional oven. After endless tries to get my flatbreads crispy without sticking to the pan and tearing apart, I settled on this method. The flatbread slides right out and looks gorgeous as one big wheel of yumminess on a breadboard. You can jazz up this flatbread with some olives, red pepper flakes, or fresh chiles. Get creative with your fillings; make this your own.

onion and herb socca

SERVES 4 TO 8

1 cup (240ml) lukewarm water

Olive oil

1 cup (160g) chickpea (garbanzo bean) flour

Natural salt (see box, page 38) and freshly ground black pepper

1/2 cup (75g) diced yellow onion

2 teaspoons finely chopped garlic (about 2 cloves)

2 tablespoons finely chopped flat-leaf parsley

1 tablespoon finely chopped thyme

Pour the water, 2 tablespoons of olive oil, the flour, and 1/2 teaspoon each of salt and pepper into your blender and pulse on low a few times until just combined. You don't want to over-process. Just get rid of the lumps.

Transfer this mixture to a bowl and let stand at room temperature for at least 30 minutes and up to 12 hours, until the flour absorbs the water and oil and the mixture has the consistency of heavy cream.

Preheat the oven to 450°F (235°C).

In a shallow frying pan over medium heat, sauté the onion in 1 tablespoon of olive oil for 10 minutes, until the onion is soft and translucent. Add the garlic and sauté for 5 minutes more, until the onion and garlic are slightly caramelized. Remove from the heat and stir in the herbs.

Grease a 9- to 10-inch (23 to 25cm) cast-iron frying pan or shallow pie plate with a tiny bit of olive oil. Spoon the onion and herb mixture into the bottom of the prepared pan and pour the batter over the top. Stir gently to disperse the onion and herbs throughout the batter.

Bake uncovered for 10 minutes. The *socca* is done when it pulls away from the sides of the pan. Remove from the oven and let cool in the pan for 5 minutes. Brush the top of the *socca* with a little bit of olive oil and season with salt and pepper. It should slide right out of the pan.

Cut into wedges and serve. *Socca* is best eaten as soon as it is made.

Welcome to raw snack nirvana! Raw foodists, vegans, health nuts, or those in the green know have been scarfing kale chips for years. Happily, these treats are now available in mainstream grocery stores. But making kale chips at home is better, less expensive, and more fun. A green, nutritious alternative to conventional come-in-a-packet snacks, kale chips are free from the carcinogens, additives, and preservatives that plague most shriveled potato chips. Dehydrated, rather than fried or baked, they retain all of their natural enzymes and nutrients. Most important, they're scrumptious.

nut-free alkaline tomato kale chips

FILLS A 1-QUART (1-LITER) BOWL FOR SNACKING

2 large bunches (400g) curly kale

1/2 cup (120ml) plus 1 tablespoon water

2 tablespoons freshly squeezed lemon juice, plus more to taste

1 cup (140g) sesame seeds (ground to a powder if using a conventional blender)

1 cup (140g) diced red bell pepper

2 tablespoons finely chopped sun-dried tomatoes

2 teaspoons diced red onion, plus more to taste

1 teaspoon natural salt (see box, page 38), plus more to taste

1/2 teaspoon yellow mustard powder

1 clove garlic

3/4 teaspoon red pepper flakes, plus more to taste (optional)

Rip the kale leaves from their stalks and wash and drain the leaves in a colander.

Throw the remaining ingredients into your high-speed blender or food processor in the order listed and blend on high or puree for 1 to 2 minutes, until thick and creamy. You want the consistency of hummus. If you're using a food processor, you may need to stop the machine periodically and scrape down the sides of the container. Tweak flavors to taste (you may like more lemon juice, onion, salt, or pepper flakes).

Transfer the kale to a large bowl and pour the mixture from the blender over the top. Using your hands, massage the leaves until they're well coated. Spread the kale pieces evenly on several dehydrator trays. Dehydrate at 115°F (46°C) for about 10 hours, until the leaves are crisp and thoroughly dried. Allow the chips to cool.

Store in a sealed container at room temperature (if you have any left over).

Like the Chock-Full Chocolate Surprise (page 60), this blend has a color that works to our advantage in getting kids to eat their greens. Fruit roll-ups, such a popular after-school snack, are typically brownish-orange, which is how these turn out. You can make this version with any fruit, or a mix, and use other leafy greens along with or instead of spinach. Kids don't suspect a thing. They'll scarf these down and nag you for more.

green smoothie fruit leathers

MAKES 2 OR 3 (14-INCH/35CM) SQUARES

1 cup (240ml) coconut water or water

2 cups (86g) firmly packed baby spinach, plus more to taste

1 cup (160g) diced fresh or frozen pineapple

1 cup (160g) diced fresh or frozen mango

1 cup (160g) fresh or frozen mixed berries

1/2 banana

Toss all of the ingredients into your blender in the order listed and blend on high for 30 to 60 seconds, until smooth and creamy. Taste, and if it's too sweet (or you just want more greens), add up to 2 more cups of spinach and blend again until smooth.

Pour about 1¹/₂ cups of the mixture onto a 14-inch (35cm) dehydrator tray covered with parchment paper or a nonstick sheet and use a rubber spatula to smooth out the mixture evenly. You don't want to be able to see through the mixture; if you can, it's too thin. Repeat with a second tray and possibly a third. Dehydrate at 115°F (46°C) for 6 to 8 hours. The leathers are done when you can peel them back easily, and they come free without sticking. If you're using parchment, they dehydrate faster.

Cut the fruit leathers into strips and store in a sealed container at room temperature for up to 2 weeks (though they never last that long).

This is a fantastic way to make fruit butter in any blender (though a high-speed machine will give you the smoothest consistency). Don't be put off by the straining. It only takes a few minutes and is totally worth it. In this recipe, resist the temptation to tweak the ingredients. The strained butter is quite mild and not too sweet. It's fabulous with ice cream, spread on baked goods, or straight out of the jar (or strainer) with a spoon, which is my preference. The pungency of the ginger winds up mostly in the juice after straining; don't miss using it to make Asian Arugula (page 93). Or, in homemade ginger ale—simply mix one part juice to one part sparkling water and sweeten to taste.

ginger-apple-pear butter

MAKES 1 CUP (265G) SAUCE

1 cup (170g) chopped pitted dates

2 ripe pears, cored and chopped

2 green apples, cored and chopped

¹⁄₄ cup (60ml) plus 2 tablespoons freshly squeezed lime juice

1¹⁄₂ tablespoons minced fresh ginger

Soak the dates in 2¹⁄₂ cups (600ml) of water for 2 hours. Place the soaked dates and their liquid into your blender and add the pears, apples, lime juice, and ginger. Blast on high for 2 to 3 minutes, until well pureed. Strain the mixture through a fine-mesh sieve set over a bowl, stirring to remove as much liquid from the pulp as possible; reserve the liquid and store in an airtight glass container in the fridge for up to 5 days. Scoop the fruit butter out of the strainer and use immediately or store in an airtight container in the fridge for up to 5 days.

This all-but-instant raw jam is a welcome alternative to traditional varieties. Chia-thickened, it tastes pretty close to conventional jams without the cooking time. Use this basic recipe with any fruit, from berries to apricots to figs. The key to the look and texture is putting half of the fruit in the blender at the end and pulsing on low speed. Blend on high and you'll get pudding! Any way you eat it—with toast, crackers, pancakes, or crepes—this is blender magic.

all-but-instant raw raspberry jam

MAKE 2 CUPS (500G)

1/4 cup (60ml) coconut water

1/2 cup (85g) firmly packed chopped pitted dates

2 tablespoons chia seeds

2 cups (320g) fresh raspberries (frozen don't work well)

Natural liquid sweetener (optional; see page 39)

Pour the coconut water into your blender and add the dates. Blast on high for 30 to 60 seconds, until the dates have broken up. Scrape down the sides of the container, then add the chia seeds and one-half of the raspberries. Pulse on low a few times, just to break up the berries. Add the remaining raspberries and pulse a few times on low to get a thick, chunky consistency. If the jam is too tart, stir in liquid sweetener to taste. Go easy, or the jam will get runny.

Chill in the fridge for 30 minutes—the chia seeds will thicken the jam and the flavors will develop. The jam will keep in the fridge for up to 4 days.

can't beet gut instincts

MAKES ABOUT 6 POUNDS (2.72KG)

¼ cup (60ml) warm water (optional)

1 tablespoon coconut sugar (optional; see page 39)

1 sachet Body Ecology culture starter (optional; see Resources, page 208)

2 heads red cabbage

6 beets, peeled

1 small red onion, peeled

1 apple

2½ tablespoons natural salt (see box, page 38), plus more to taste

3 tablespoons grated fresh horseradish (not horseradish sauce)

3 tablespoons minced fresh ginger

2 to 3 tablespoons finely chopped garlic

¼ cup (60ml) plus 2 tablespoons freshly squeezed lemon juice

1 teaspoon finely grated lemon zest

If using the culture starter (see note, opposite page), combine the warm water and sugar in a bowl and stir until the sugar dissolves. Stir in the culture starter and let sit for at least 20 minutes.

Remove the outer leaves from the cabbages. Wash these leaves and set them aside. (You will use the outer leaves to pack and seal the jars.) In the bowl of a food processor fitted with the S blade or shredder disc, shred the cabbage, beets, onion, and apple. In a large mixing bowl, combine the shredded veggies with the salt. Using your hands, massage the salt into the vegetables for 3 to 4 minutes. This will begin to draw the liquid from the vegetables (the mixture will reduce significantly in volume). Add the horseradish, ginger, garlic, lemon juice, and lemon zest. Add more salt to taste. (This makes a delicious salad at this point.)

Measure out 3 cups (660g) of the vegetables along with some of the juices and put it into your blender. Pulse just a few times, until you have a soupy pulp. (You may have to add a tiny bit of water.) Add the blended veggies back into the shredded mixture and stir well.

Pack the vegetables as tightly as possible into airtight mason jars or stainless steel canisters using a potato masher or heavy spoon to push the vegetables down. Get out as much of the air as possible. Leave about 2 inches at the top of each container for expansion. Roll 2 or 3 cabbage leaves into tight "cigars" and place them on top of the vegetables to fill the remaining space. Seal the containers and let them sit at room temperature (70°F/21°C) or slightly warmer (which accelerates fermentation) for at least 4 days, but preferably 7 days. The key is to have a stable temperature, so if you don't have an area that qualifies, wrap the jars in towels and place them in an insulated or thermal chest. In warm weather, the vegetables culture in 3 to 4 days. Don't let the jars sit in direct sunlight. If you're using screw-top lids, open the jars halfway through fermentation to let gas escape. You may also have to pour out a bit of the liquid if it rises above the level of the shredded vegetables.

Taste the vegetables after 3 or 4 days (you should hear them bubbling), and keep tasting every day until they are just right for your preference. Once the veggies are ready, place the containers in the fridge to slow the fermentation. The cultured vegetables will keep in the fridge for up to 8 months.

There are many pros to cultured vegetables. This delicious combination is my favorite. It is PROnounced in zesty flavor, PROlific in live enzymes and life-affirming bacteria, and not PROhibitively expensive. Eating a half-cup of this mix with most meals has literally changed my life, giving me improved digestion and better health. Enjoy these as a quick snack or an accompaniment to cooked dishes, or add them to salads and wraps. Using the starter is optional. I generally don't use it; however, it does get fermentation going rapidly and assures uniform results from batch to batch. Seven days is how long I typically ferment before I PROclaim this ready!

CHAPTER 5

salads

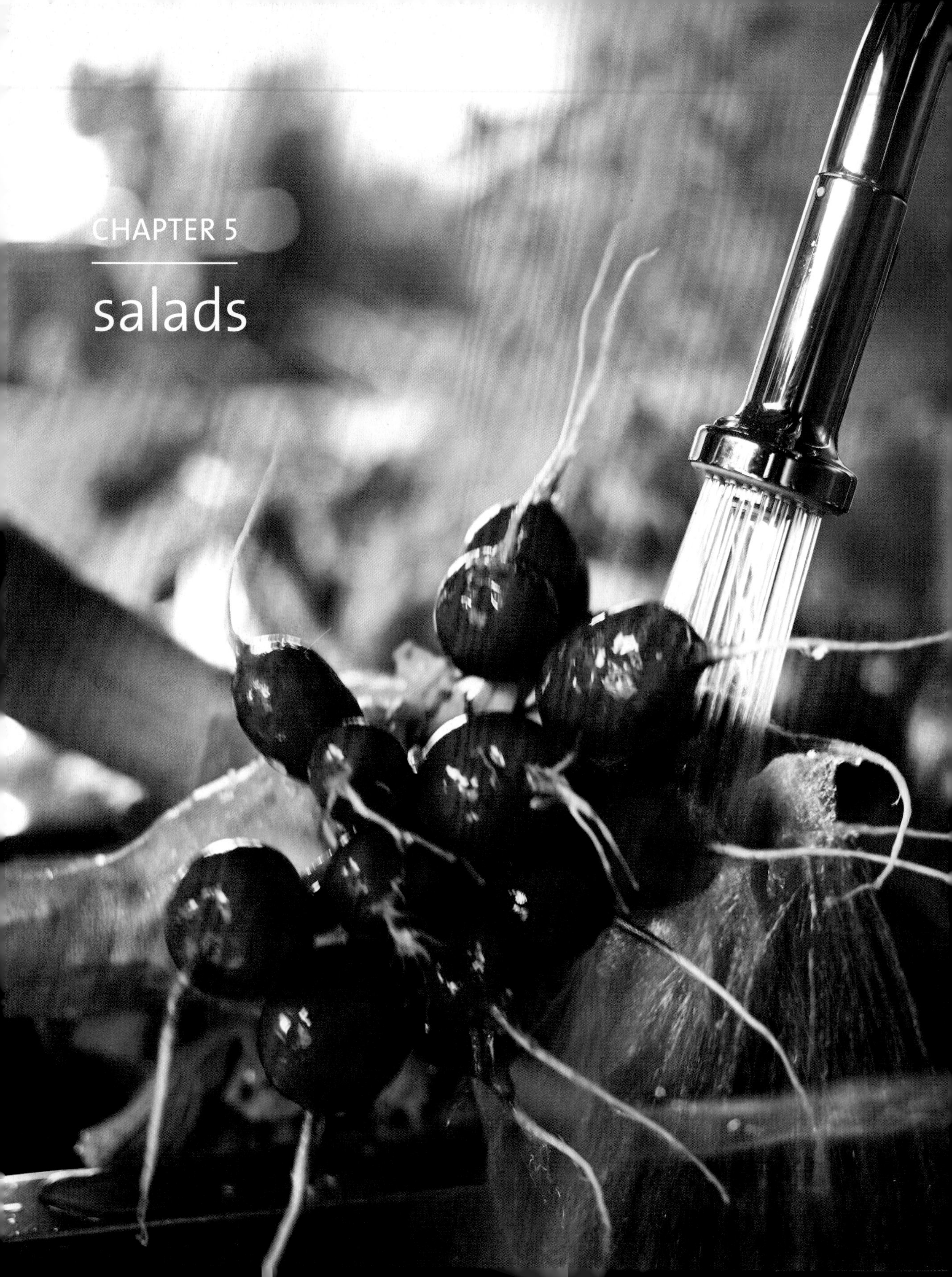

This vegan spin on classic potato salad strikes a pleasing balance between sweet and tangy flavors and creamy and crunchy textures. The recipe is really adaptable, too. Swap out the broccoli for some cucumber, or replace the red bell pepper with a yellow one. I've thrown this salad together with all kinds of raw veggies to rave reviews. And the salad tastes even better the next day. If you use a traditional egg-based mayo, you may not need the vinegar or salt. Whichever way you go, these spuds are definitely not duds, and this salad is hard to quit eating.

creamy and crunchy spuds

SERVES 8; THE DRESSING MAKES 1³/₄ CUPS (410G)

potatoes

2³/₄ pounds (1.2kg) potatoes, peeled and cut into 1-inch (2.5cm) cubes

1 tablespoon natural salt (see box, page 38), plus more to taste

1 bunch green onions (white and green parts), finely chopped

¹/₂ cup (75g) diced red onion

1 cup (140g) diced red bell pepper

1 cup (132g) diced celery (about 4 large ribs)

1 cup (150g) julienned broccoli stalks or commercial broccoli slaw, or 1 cup (145g) peeled, seeded, and diced cucumber

1 bunch flat-leaf parsley, finely chopped

Freshly ground black pepper

dressing

1¹/₃ cups (310g) I-Use-It-in-Everything Raw Mayo (page 198), or your preferred brand of mayonnaise

2¹/₂ tablespoons Dijon mustard, plus more to taste

2¹/₂ tablespoons stone-ground mustard, plus more to taste

1 teaspoon apple cider vinegar, plus more to taste

¹/₄ teaspoon natural salt, plus more to taste

To cook the potatoes, place them in a large pot and add cold water to cover. Add the salt and bring the water to a boil over high heat. Reduce the heat to medium and simmer the potatoes for about 8 minutes, just until fork-tender. (You don't want to overcook your potatoes, or you will end up with a mash rather than a chunky salad.) Drain the potatoes, rinse them with cold water, and drain them again thoroughly. Allow them to cool completely.

To make the dressing, put the mayonnaise, mustards, vinegar, and salt into your blender. Blend on high for about 1 minute, until smooth and creamy. Tweak flavors to taste (you may like more mustard, vinegar, or salt).

To assemble the salad, transfer the cooled potatoes to a large bowl. Add the green onions, red onion, red bell pepper, celery, broccoli, and parsley. Pour on the dressing and fold in gently, keeping the potatoes as intact as possible. Season with salt and pepper to taste. Serve chilled or at room temperature. The salad will keep in the fridge for up to 5 days.

No culinary repertoire is complete without a killer Greek. The Switzerland of salads, this simple dish seems to please everybody with its light, refreshing flavors. I must admit that the socialist in me takes over when I create salads—I want to distribute a bit of every ingredient with every forkful. This version contains tons of fresh herbs and just the right variety of vegetables to achieve full flavor with every chomp.

glowing greek

SERVES 6 AS A STARTER, 4 AS A MAIN; THE DRESSING MAKES ABOUT 1 CUP (240ML)

dressing

1 tablespoon red wine vinegar

1 tablespoon freshly squeezed lemon juice

1 teaspoon finely chopped flat-leaf parsley

1 teaspoon finely chopped thyme

1 teaspoon finely chopped oregano

1/2 teaspoon Dijon mustard

1 teaspoon minced garlic (about 1 clove)

1/2 teaspoon natural salt (see box, page 38)

1/8 teaspoon freshly ground black pepper

1/2 cup (120ml) cold-pressed extra-virgin olive oil

salad

2 cups (300g) seeded and roughly chopped tomato

2 cups (70g) firmly packed romaine lettuce (2 or 3 large leaves), cut into ribbons

1 cup (145g) peeled, seeded, and roughly chopped cucumber

1 cup (140g) diced red bell pepper

1 cup (140g) diced yellow bell pepper

1/2 cup (50g) sliced red onion

1/2 cup (65g) pitted, halved kalamata olives

Macadamia "Feta" (page 73), or regular feta, crumbled, to garnish (optional)

Natural salt and freshly ground black pepper

To make the dressing, put the vinegar, lemon juice, herbs, mustard, garlic, salt, and pepper into your blender. Blend on low for 10 to 20 seconds, until well combined. With the blender running, pour the oil through the lid opening slowly, increasing the blender's speed to emulsify. Set aside.

To assemble the salad, in a serving bowl, toss the tomatoes, lettuce, cucumber, peppers, onion, and olives with 1/2 cup (120ml) of the dressing. Add additional dressing to taste and toss again. Serve topped with crumbled feta and a sprinkle of salt and pepper. Pass any remaining dressing at the table.

A good Caesar salad just has to be rich and creamy, with the right amount of crunch, or so my dad opines. This tangy and delicious vegan version delivers on all three, and you'll never miss the egg or the anchovies (dulse, a sea vegetable, replicates the taste of the fish). Dad says it's the best ever. Hey, I haven't sampled every Caesar on the planet, but this one is pretty darn good.

twisted caesar pleaser

SERVES 8 AS A STARTER, 4 AS A MAIN; THE DRESSING MAKES 1¹/₂ CUPS (360ML)

dressing

¹/₄ cup (60ml) plus 2 tablespoons unsweetened almond milk (strained if homemade)

¹/₄ cup (60ml) cold-pressed extra-virgin olive oil

1 tablespoon freshly squeezed lemon juice

¹/₄ cup (30g) blanched raw almonds, soaked (see page 22)

2 tablespoons pine nuts, soaked (see page 22)

2 tablespoons sunflower seeds

1 tablespoon capers, drained and rinsed

1 tablespoon white miso paste

1 teaspoon Dijon mustard

1¹/₂ teaspoons wheat-free tamari

2 teaspoons minced garlic (about 2 cloves)

¹/₄ teaspoon natural salt (see box, page 38)

croutons

¹/₄ cup (60ml) olive oil

¹/₂ teaspoon dried parsley

¹/₂ teaspoon dried rosemary

¹/₂ teaspoon dried thyme

¹/₂ teaspoon dried oregano

¹/₂ teaspoon garlic powder

¹/₂ teaspoon onion powder

¹/₄ teaspoon natural salt

¹/₈ teaspoon freshly ground black pepper

2 cups (64g) cubed gluten-free or regular bread (¹/₂-inch/1cm cubes; about 4 slices)

salad

4 heads romaine lettuce, roughly chopped

2 cups (60g) baby spinach, cut into ribbons

2 cups (290g) peeled, seeded, and diced cucumber (about 2 medium)

¹/₂ cup (75g) diced red onion

2 avocados, pitted, peeled, and diced

1 to 2 teaspoons dried dulse flakes (optional; see Resources, page 209)

¹/₂ cup (43g) Pine Nut "Parmesan" (page 73) or regular parmesan

Natural salt and freshly ground black pepper

To make the dressing, throw all of the ingredients into your blender and blast on high for 1 to 2 minutes, until smooth and creamy. Chill in the fridge.

To make the croutons, preheat the oven to 300°F/150°C. Put the olive oil, dried herbs, garlic and onion powders, salt, and pepper into your blender and pulse on low for 10 to 20 seconds, until combined. Place the bread cubes in a bowl and drizzle the oil and herb mixture over top. Toss the bread cubes until evenly coated and transfer to a baking sheet. Bake for 4 minutes, toss the cubes, and bake for another 4 minutes. Remove the croutons from the oven and let them cool.

To assemble the salad, toss together the romaine, spinach, cucumber, onion, and avocados in a bowl. Sprinkle on the dulse flakes and half of the "parmesan." Add half of the dressing and toss. Season with salt and pepper to taste and top with the croutons and the rest of the "parmesan." Pass the remaining dressing at the table.

This little gem was a happy accident. After my mate Denise and I made a batch of Ginger-Apple-Pear Butter (page 82), our friend Mika sampled the leftover liquid and thought it would make an amazing Japanese-style salad dressing. Excited by her inspiration, we all starting riffing and threw together this salad with fresh ingredients on hand. The results were magic. Some things are just meant to be.

asian arugula

SERVES 6 AS A STARTER, 4 AS A MAIN; THE DRESSING MAKES 3/4 CUP (180ML)

dressing

1/2 cup (120ml) of the liquid strained from Ginger-Apple-Pear Butter (page 82)

2 tablespoons wheat-free tamari or soy sauce

1/4 cup (60ml) cold-pressed extra-virgin olive oil

salad

10 cups (220g) loosely packed arugula

1/2 cucumber, peeled and diced

3 small radishes, cut into extremely thin half-moons

6 ounces (170g) firm tofu

1 avocado, pitted, peeled, and cut into wedges

1/3 cup (47g) sliced or blanched slivered raw almonds

Natural salt (see box, page 38)

To make the dressing, put the ginger-apple-pear liquid, tamari, and olive oil into your blender and blast on high for 10 to 20 seconds, until well combined. Set aside.

To make the salad, throw the arugula leaves into a large salad bowl. Add the cucumber and radishes, and then crumble the tofu over the top, scattered like bits of feta. Add the dressing, toss, and then top with the avocado and almonds. Season with salt and serve immediately, before the arugula wilts.

My mother *loves* this dressing. The first time she tasted it, she insisted that I scrape out the blender carriage with absolute precision to retrieve every last drop. Not content with my clearly inferior spatula, she became possessed and proceeded to maneuver her tongue into the blender carriage with the dexterity of a contortionist! This, from the woman who raised me never to put my elbows on the table, to lay my knife and fork diagonally across my plate, and to ask politely whether I might leave the table. Needless to say, this salad is gooood.

pear and candied walnut with raspberry vinaigrette

SERVES 6 TO 8; THE DRESSING MAKES 1¹/₂ CUPS (360ML)

candied walnuts

2 cups (220g) raw walnuts

¹/₃ cup (80ml) pure maple syrup

Pinch of natural salt (see box, page 38)

2 teaspoons water

dressing

3 tablespoons grapeseed oil or light olive oil

1¹/₂ tablespoons apple cider vinegar

1¹/₂ tablespoons freshly squeezed lemon juice

1¹/₂ teaspoons pure maple syrup

¹/₄ teaspoon natural salt

¹/₈ teaspoon freshly ground black pepper

1 cup (160g) raspberries, fresh or defrosted frozen

salad

4 cups (108g) loosely packed baby spinach

4 cups (100g) loosely packed mixed leafy greens or arugula

2 pears, cored and sliced thinly in half moons

To make the candied walnuts, preheat the oven to 350°F (180°C). Line a baking sheet with parchment paper.

Place the walnuts on the prepared baking sheet and toast for 10 minutes, until fragrant.

Combine the maple syrup and salt in a saucepan over medium-low heat. Bring to a boil, stirring constantly, and let bubble for 5 minutes. Stir in the water and the walnuts hot from the oven. When the walnuts are coated and have started to caramelize and the liquid has evaporated (after 3 to 4 minutes), the maple syrup will crystallize. Place the nuts back on the baking sheet to cool and harden for 15 minutes.

To make the dressing, put all of the ingredients into your blender in the order listed and puree on medium for 30 to 60 seconds, until smooth and creamy. Strain the dressing through a fine-mesh sieve and discard the seeds.

To assemble the salad, in a serving bowl, toss together the greens and pears and add half of the dressing. Sprinkle with 1 cup of the walnuts and add more dressing to taste. Pass the remaining dressing and candied walnuts at the table.

The French dressing I grew up eating in Australia is what Americans call vinaigrette and bears no resemblance to the creamy orange concoction that greeted me on the first salad I ordered in the States. "Yuk!" I thought, smugly determined never to dip my discerning snout into *that* again. My love for "that weird orange dressing" came as a slow burn. But when I sampled my friend Geoffrey's famous blend, I tumbled at the first bite.

In this recipe, I've "Blender Girled" (as Geoffrey puts it) his secret sauce by featuring tarragon, chile peppers, liquid aminos, and maple syrup; the results are magnificent. Geoffrey says this takes him back to his childhood. Many of my American friends say the same. Hailing from another hemisphere where we wrestle crocodiles, I can't share the memories, but perhaps you can. The vegetable combinations in this salad complement the dressing beautifully, and it is all so easy to make.

earthy french

SERVES 6 AS A STARTER, 4 AS A MAIN; THE DRESSING MAKES 1 1/3 CUPS (320ML)

dressing

1 cup (240ml) cold-pressed extra-virgin olive oil

1/4 cup (60ml) apple cider vinegar

1/4 cup (60ml) I'll Have Ketchup with That (page 196), or your preferred brand of ketchup

1 tablespoon freshly squeezed lemon juice

2 teaspoons pure maple syrup

1 clove garlic, plus more to taste

1/2 teaspoon Bragg liquid aminos (see page 132)

3/4 teaspoon dried tarragon

1/4 teaspoon red pepper flakes

3/4 teaspoon natural salt (see box, page 38)

1/2 teaspoon freshly ground black pepper

salad

1 large head romaine lettuce, torn

1 large cucumber, peeled and chopped

2 large tomatoes, chopped

1 (15-ounce/425g) can chickpeas or cannellini beans, rinsed and drained well

6 white button mushrooms, sliced

2 avocados, pitted, peeled, and sliced

2 radishes, sliced very thinly, or 4 thinly sliced red onion rounds, broken up

1 teaspoon freshly squeezed lemon juice, plus more to taste

Natural salt and freshly ground black pepper

To make the dressing, throw all of the ingredients into your blender and blast on high for 30 to 60 seconds, until rich and creamy. Tweak garlic to taste. Refrigerate the dressing until ready to serve.

To assemble the salad, in a serving bowl, combine all of the ingredients. Add the dressing to your preference and toss well. Tweak lemon juice to taste, season with salt and pepper, and pass the remaining dressing at the table.

I think of this salad dressing as the culinary equivalent of my little black dress—a staple that gets pulled out, works for most occasions, and never goes out of style. I love the peppery notes in this dressing, but any blend of herbs and greens can yield spectacular results. This lean green dressing machine will transform even the most tragic mound of lettuce from drab to fab. People swoon when they taste it. Many a friend has exclaimed in the midst of a euphoric bite, "Oh, I could just gobble this up with a spoon!" I have done that, and also licked it out of the blender carriage before it even had the chance to get dressed up.

green queen

SERVES 8 AS A STARTER, 6 AS A MAIN; THE DRESSING MAKES 1½ CUPS (360ML)

dressing

¾ cup (180ml) cold-pressed extra-virgin olive oil

¼ cup (60ml) freshly squeezed lemon juice, plus more to taste

1 bunch flat-leaf parsley leaves, chopped

1 bunch cilantro, chopped

½ bunch chopped chives

⅓ cup (40g) blanched raw almonds or ¼ cup (35g) raw sunflower seeds, soaked (see page 22)

½ avocado, pitted and peeled

1 clove garlic, minced, plus more to taste

1 teaspoon apple cider vinegar

½ teaspoon natural salt (see box, page 38), plus more to taste

½ cup (120ml) water, plus more as needed

salad

2 zucchini

8 cups (200g) mixed leafy greens, like baby spinach, arugula, or micro greens

¼ head purple cabbage, cored and shredded

2 cups (300g) julienned broccoli stalks or commercial broccoli slaw, or 2 cups (290g) peeled, seeded, and diced or julienned cucumber

2 avocados, pitted, peeled, and sliced

1 bunch green onions (white and green parts), finely chopped

1 cup (160g) roughly chopped raw almonds

¼ cup (35g) hemp, sunflower, or pumpkin seeds

Natural salt and freshly ground black pepper

To make the dressing, put all of the ingredients into your blender and puree on high for about 1 minute, until smooth and creamy. Tweak flavors to taste (you might want more lemon juice, garlic, or salt). This dressing should have the consistency of thin mayo, but add a little more water to thin it out if you prefer. It can be stored in an airtight container in the fridge for up to 5 days.

To assemble the salad, shave the zucchini lengthwise into strips with a vegetable peeler, discarding the seedy core. In a large serving bowl, toss together the zucchini strips, greens, cabbage, broccoli, avocados, green onions, almonds, and seeds. Add the dressing to your preference and toss well. Season with salt and pepper and pass any remaining dressing at the table.

If you think you can't stomach kale in a salad, this sensational dressing might just change your mind. I've converted many a naysayer with this glorious blend, and I don't intend to stop now. Yes, it really is that good. The secret is in the massage. Kale is bitter by nature, so you have to get touchy-feely to bring out her sweetness. Get your hands in there and give that kale some love. This salad will wow you with every twist and crunch.

magic mango massage

SERVES 6 AS A STARTER, 4 AS A MAIN; THE DRESSING MAKES ABOUT 2 CUPS (480ML)

dressing

1/2 cup (120ml) coconut water

1 cup (160g) chopped fresh or defrosted frozen mango (about 1 large mango)

1 tablespoon freshly squeezed lime juice

1 teaspoon finely grated lime zest

1 teaspoon finely chopped green serrano chile

11/2 teaspoons minced ginger

1/2 teaspoon Bragg liquid aminos (see page 132), wheat-free tamari, or soy sauce

1 clove garlic

1 teaspoon finely chopped red onion

2 tablespoons finely chopped cilantro

2 tablespoons finely chopped mint

1/2 teaspoon natural salt (see box, page 38)

salad

2 bunches green or red curly kale

1/4 cup (60ml) cold-pressed extra-virgin olive oil

2 tablespoons freshly squeezed lemon juice

3 tablespoons chopped cilantro

3 tablespoons chopped mint

1 ripe mango, sliced or cubed

1 large or 2 small avocados, pitted, peeled, and sliced or cubed

2 tablespoons sliced or blanched slivered raw almonds

Natural salt (optional)

To make the dressing, throw all of the ingredients into your blender and blast on high for about 1 minute, until smooth and creamy. Chill in the fridge until ready to serve.

To assemble the salad, rip the kale leaves from their stalks and tear the leaves into pieces. In a small bowl, combine the olive oil and lemon juice. Add the kale to a serving bowl and pour the oil mixture over the top. Using your hands, massage the oil into the kale for about 1 minute, until well coated. Add the dressing, cilantro, and mint and massage again. Add the mango, avocado, and almonds, and toss gently. Season with salt and serve immediately.

"If I wanted a taste of the ocean, I would have gone for a swim. Seaweed is for sushi!" Perhaps you agree with my dear dad. But, like him, you may quickly recant upon tasting this salad. Sea vegetables are so rich in vitamins and alkalizing minerals like calcium that I include them in as many of my dishes as possible. But they scare off some people. The trick is to mix them with other "socially acceptable" veggies, and then top them with a killer dressing. This divine citrus blend works well on all kinds of salads, but it pairs beautifully with these veggies to make dining on the sea pretty darn tasty.

citrus sea slaw

SERVES 4 AS A STARTER, 2 AS A MAIN; THE DRESSING MAKES 1¹/₄ CUPS (300ML)

dressing

¹/₂ cup (120ml) freshly squeezed orange juice

3 tablespoons cold-pressed extra-virgin olive oil

2 tablespoons expeller-pressed sesame oil

1 tablespoon plus 2 teaspoons apple cider vinegar

2 tablespoons tahini

1 teaspoon wheat-free tamari, soy sauce, or Bragg liquid aminos (see page 132)

1 teaspoon finely grated orange zest

2 teaspoons minced ginger

2 tablespoons pure maple syrup, plus more to taste

¹/₂ teaspoon freshly squeezed lime juice, plus more to taste

¹/₄ teaspoon finely grated lime zest, plus more to taste

³/₄ teaspoon natural salt (see box, page 38), plus more to taste

¹/₈ teaspoon red pepper flakes, plus more to taste

salad

2 tablespoons hijiki (see Resources, page 208)

¹/₂ cup (15g) dried arame (see Resources, page 208)

2 cups (50g) mixed leafy greens

¹/₈ head red cabbage, shredded

1 large English (hothouse) cucumber, peeled and julienned

1 carrot, peeled and julienned

¹/₂ cup (40g) julienned jicama

8 water chestnuts, drained and julienned

2 tablespoons sunflower seeds

1 tablespoon freshly squeezed lime juice

¹/₂ teaspoon natural salt

To make the dressing, throw all of the ingredients into your blender and blast on high for 1 to 2 minutes, until smooth and creamy. Tweak flavors to taste (you may like more maple syrup, lime juice or zest, salt, or pepper flakes). Chill in the fridge until ready to serve.

To assemble the salad, soak the hijiki in 2 cups (480ml) of water for 20 to 30 minutes, until tender. Soak the arame in 2 cups (480ml) of water for 5 to 10 minutes, until tender. Drain and rinse the hijiki and arame. In a serving bowl, combine the hijiki, arame, greens, cabbage, cucumber, carrot, jicama, water chestnuts, sunflower seeds, lime juice, and salt. Stir in the dressing and tweak flavors to taste (you may want more lime juice or salt). Serve immediately.

My friend Geoffrey is a salad alchemist and we created this warm salad together. Yes, it requires some time, but it's oh so worth it. The sweetness of the caramelized onions and roasted tomatoes blend together with the smokiness of the maple syrup, the heat of the red pepper flakes, and the acidity of the lemon juice and apple cider vinegar in a dressing (or pasta sauce) that's to die for. Combine it with the peppery notes of the arugula and the earthiness of the lentils and you've got a satisfying winner. Our friend Bernhard ate three servings and said, "Wow! Is it bad that I think this tastes like BBQ?" Nope. This is delicious comfort food, and you won't miss the meat.

mental for lentils

SERVES 8 AS A MAIN

1 pound (450g) Roma tomatoes

6 cloves garlic, unpeeled

4 sprigs thyme

Natural salt (see box, page 38) and freshly ground black pepper

2 cups (380g) dried green lentils

3 yellow, white, or red onions, sliced into 1/4-inch (6mm) rings

Olive oil

1/4 cup (60ml) balsamic vinegar

4 cups (640g) diced carrots

4 cups (540g) diced zucchini

1/4 cup (12g) finely chopped flat-leaf parsley

1 1/2 tablespoons grainy Dijon mustard

Freshly squeezed lemon juice

2 teaspoons pure maple syrup, plus more to taste

1 teaspoon Bragg liquid aminos (see page 132)

1/2 teaspoon apple cider vinegar, plus more to taste

1/4 teaspoon dried red pepper flakes, plus more to taste

10 cups (220g) loosely packed arugula

Preheat the oven to 450°F (235°C). Line a baking sheet with parchment paper.

Place the tomatoes, garlic, and thyme sprigs on the prepared baking sheet. Season with 1/8 teaspoon each of salt and pepper. Roast for approximately 30 minutes, until the tomato skins start to brown and the flesh is soft; it's okay if they collapse. Set the tomatoes aside to cool, reserve the garlic, and discard the thyme sprigs.

In a pot over high heat, cover the lentils with 8 cups (1.9l) of water and season with 1/2 teaspoon of salt. Bring to a boil, reduce the heat to medium, and simmer for about 12 minutes, until just al dente. Drain the lentils and allow them to cool.

In a large frying pan over medium-high heat, toss the onions with 2 tablespoons of olive oil and 1/4 teaspoon each of salt and pepper. Sauté the onions for 8 minutes. Add 1/8 teaspoon of salt and stir; reduce the heat to medium and cook for about 15 minutes more, stirring occasionally, until the onions start to caramelize and have shrunk to half their size. Stir in the balsamic vinegar, reduce the heat to low, and simmer until the onions have absorbed the balsamic, about 15 minutes. Transfer the onion mixture to a bowl and set aside.

In the same frying pan, heat 2 tablespoons of olive oil over medium heat. Add the carrots and sauté for 3 to 4 minutes, until slightly tender. Add the zucchini and increase the heat to medium-high. Add $1/8$ teaspoon of salt and continue cooking for 3 to 5 minutes, until the vegetables are slightly browned but still al dente. Remove the pan from the heat and stir in the parsley.

To make the dressing, put $1/2$ cup of olive oil into your blender. Squeeze the roasted garlic pulp out of the skins and add it to the blender along with the onion mixture and the roasted tomatoes. Add the mustard, 2 teaspoons of lemon juice, the maple syrup, liquid aminos, apple cider vinegar, pepper flakes, and $1/4$ teaspoon of salt. Puree on high for 1 to 2 minutes, until the mixture is thick and well combined. Tweak flavors to taste (you may like more maple syrup, vinegar, pepper flakes, or salt).

To assemble the salad, in a large serving bowl, toss the arugula with 2 tablespoons of olive oil, 2 tablespoons of lemon juice, and a pinch of salt. Add the lentils, the carrot and zucchini mixture, $1^{1/2}$ cups (365ml) of the dressing, and 2 tablespoons of lemon juice, or more to taste. Season with salt and pepper, toss well, and serve immediately, passing the extra dressing at the table.

soups

For a simple, impressive, and downright delicious soup, you can't surpass this rich and creamy blend. This is the recipe my friends request most. When they come over for dinner, they always ask in anticipation, "Are you making the cauliflower soup?" Because you can literally make this blend on demand in about forty minutes, I always keep a head of cauliflower in my fridge. A scoop of cooked grain or a piece of crusty bread makes this soup a meal. It freezes nicely, too.

The secret ingredient is the nuts, which, when blended with the cauliflower, create silky texture, a rich flavor, and an intoxicating aroma. It's staggering that something so easy delivers so complex a result. Just be sure to soak the nuts and puree the soup really well to get the consistency that my friends proclaim "liquid air." This is a *blendsation* that will make you look like a gourmet chef!

creamy cauliflower

SERVES 6 AS A STARTER, 4 AS A MAIN

2 tablespoons olive oil

2 teaspoons chopped garlic (about 2 cloves), plus more to taste

2 cups (200g) chopped leeks (white parts only, from 2 or 3 leeks)

Natural salt (see box, page 38)

1 head cauliflower, chopped

7 cups (1.65l) vegetable broth (see page 115)

1/4 cup (35g) raw unsalted cashews or 1/4 cup (35g) blanched slivered raw almonds, soaked (see page 22)

3 tablespoons chopped chives or a grating of nutmeg (optional; choose one, not both), to garnish

In a large saucepan, heat the oil over medium heat and sauté the garlic, leeks, and 1/4 teaspoon of salt for about 3 minutes, until the vegetables are soft. Add the cauliflower and sauté for another minute. Add the vegetable broth, increase the heat to high, and bring just to a boil. Reduce the heat to medium and simmer for about 30 minutes, until the cauliflower is completely tender. Stir the mix periodically and mash the cauliflower with a wooden spoon.

Remove the saucepan from the heat and allow the soup to cool slightly; stir in the nuts. Pour the soup into your blender in batches and puree on high for 1 to 2 minutes, until smooth and creamy. (Remember to remove the plastic cap in the blender top and cover the opening with a kitchen towel so steam can escape while you blend.) Return the soup to the saucepan and warm it over low heat. Stir in salt to taste.

To serve, ladle the soup into bowls and garnish with either chopped chives or grated nutmeg.

what is a grain ball?

I like to supplement a bowl of blended soup with a scoop of cooked grain (day-old is best, as it sticks together). I prefer the protein-rich grains—quinoa, amaranth, and millet (they're alkaline, too). But use any grains you like—brown rice, buckwheat, or (if you're not gluten-free) pearl barley. Try cooking grains in vegetable broth or coconut milk, and/or adding some ginger, garlic, sea vegetables, herbs, and spices for an added boost of flavor.

I love tomato soup, and I typically roast my tomatoes to get a deep, rich flavor and sweetness. Roasting takes some time, so I've left that step out of this recipe, which you can get on the table in about forty minutes. As fresh tomatoes vary greatly in quality and flavor, I give them backup. Blending in canned and sun-dried tomatoes guarantees depth of flavor. The other high-taste components—the peppers and macadamias—more than hold up their end. But if you want to go for ultimate flavor, roast your tomatoes and toss in some fresh basil in the final minutes of cooking. This soup is also delicious served cold, especially in the summertime. Hot or cold, roasted or not, this basic tomato offering hits the sweet spot.

rich but simple tomato

SERVES 6 AS A STARTER, 4 AS A MAIN

1 tablespoon olive oil

2 tablespoons finely chopped garlic (about 6 cloves)

1 large red onion, roughly chopped

Natural salt (see box, page 38)

1 red bell pepper, seeded and roughly chopped

8 Roma tomatoes, roughly chopped

1 (28-ounce/794g) can unsalted diced or crushed tomatoes

1 teaspoon chopped sun-dried tomatoes, or 1 tablespoon tomato paste

4 cups (960ml) vegetable broth (see page 115)

1/4 cup (35g) raw unsalted macadamias

Freshly ground black pepper

1/4 cup (7g) chopped basil

In a large saucepan, heat the oil over medium heat. Add the garlic, onion, and 1/4 teaspoon of salt and saute for 5 minutes, until the onion is translucent. Add the bell pepper and fresh tomatoes and sauté for 5 minutes more. Stir in the canned tomatoes and their juices, the sun-dried tomatoes, and the vegetable broth. Increase the heat to high and bring just to a boil, then reduce the heat to medium and simmer for 30 minutes.

Remove the saucepan from the heat and allow the soup to cool slightly; stir in the macadamias. Pour the soup into your blender in batches and puree on high for about 1 minute, until smooth and creamy. (Remember to remove the plastic cap in the blender top and cover the opening with a kitchen towel so steam can escape while you blend.) Return the soup to the saucepan and warm it over low heat. Season with salt and pepper and serve garnished with the basil.

This vegan variant on cream of mushroom is a prime example of how a partially blended soup can deliver spectacular results. To avoid having to make a roux, I blend the base for creaminess, but not the mushrooms. This delivers a dairy-inspired experience, and the added hints of nutmeg and cayenne make your tongue tingle and your belly dance. I've deliberately used button mushrooms here to make the dish affordable and accessible, but using a variety of mushrooms, such as cremini, portobello, shiitake, chanterelles, and porcini, would kick this up to "wow."

mushroom magic

SERVES 8 AS A STARTER, 4 AS A MAIN

$1/4$ cup (60ml) olive oil or grapeseed oil

2 cups (200g) chopped leeks (white and paler green parts from 2 or 3 leeks)

Natural salt (see box, page 38)

2 teaspoons minced garlic (about 2 cloves)

12 ounces (340g) firm tofu

$5^1/_2$ cups (1.3l) vegetable broth (see page 115)

8 cups (720g) white button mushrooms, diced

Freshly ground white or black pepper

2 tablespoons wheat-free tamari or soy sauce

2 tablespoons cornstarch, arrowroot, or kuzu-root powder

2 tablespoons water

$1/_8$ teaspoon ground nutmeg

Tiny pinch of cayenne pepper

In a large saucepan, heat 2 tablespoons of the oil over medium heat. Add the leeks and a pinch of salt, and sauté for about 5 minutes, until the leeks are soft and translucent. Add the garlic and sauté for 2 minutes more. Transfer the leeks to your blender and add the tofu and $1^1/_2$ cups (360ml) of the vegetable broth. Blast on high for about 1 minute, until smooth and creamy.

In the same saucepan, heat the remaining 2 tablespoons of oil over medium-low heat. Add the mushrooms and a pinch of white pepper and sauté for 3 to 5 minutes, until the mushrooms are softened. Add the tofu mixture and the remaining 4 cups (960ml) of broth to the saucepan. Increase the heat to high, bring the soup just to a boil, and then reduce the heat to medium. Add the tamari and simmer for 10 minutes.

In a small bowl, combine the cornstarch and water, and then slowly stir the mixture into the soup. Cook for 5 minutes more, stirring, until the soup thickens. Stir in the nutmeg and cayenne, season to taste with salt and pepper, and serve.

This is one of the most popular recipes on my website because it's ludicrously easy, absolutely scrumptious, and freezes well. Be sure to soak your nuts and blend thoroughly to ensure the smoothest consistency. Resist the urge to add more spinach as it can make your soup watery. I usually serve this soup with a scoop of cooked grain (see page 113), but you may prefer some crusty bread. This creamy greeny seduces even the most devoted of spinach haters. Popeye would be proud.

dream of spinach

SERVES 6 AS A STARTER, 4 AS A MAIN

1 head garlic	1/4 cup (33g) diced celery (about 1 rib)	2 cups (86g) firmly packed baby spinach
1 tablespoon olive oil	1 cup (135g) diced zucchini	1/4 cup (35g) blanched slivered raw almonds or 1/4 cup (35g) raw unsalted cashews, soaked (see page 22)
1/4 cup (20g) finely chopped green onions (mostly the white part)	1/4 cup (12g) finely chopped flat-leaf parsley	
1 cup (100g) sliced red onion	4 cups (960ml) vegetable broth (see page 115)	Freshly ground black pepper
Natural salt (see box, page 38)		

Preheat the oven to 350°F (180°C).

Cut off the top of the head of garlic, wrap the bulb in aluminum foil, and roast it on a baking sheet for 30 to 40 minutes, until tender. Allow the bulb to cool and then squeeze the garlic pulp out of the husks. This should yield 2 tablespoons or more of roasted garlic. Set aside.

Heat the oil over medium-high heat in a large saucepan. Add the green onions, red onion, and 1/4 teaspoon of salt and saute for 5 minutes, until the onions are translucent. Add the celery, zucchini, and parsley and sauté for 5 minutes more. Stir in the roasted garlic and the vegetable broth. Increase the heat to high and bring just to a boil. Reduce the heat to medium and simmer for 10 minutes. Add the spinach and simmer for 5 minutes more, until the leaves are just tender. Remove the saucepan from the heat and allow the soup to cool somewhat. Stir in the nuts.

Pour the soup into your blender in batches and puree on high for 1 to 2 minutes, until smooth and creamy. (Remember to remove the plastic cap in the blender top and cover the opening with a kitchen towel so steam can escape while you blend.) Return the soup to the saucepan and warm over medium-low heat. Season to taste with salt and pepper and serve.

I have to admit, when I love a movie or a song, I play it over and over until it makes everyone around me insane. But I find myself singing this squash-soup song again and again . . . and no one's tired of it yet! I have served this soup at many dinner parties, and countless satisfied diners have told me they could have happily kept inhaling the first course. With a velvety texture and warm undertones of ginger, the bright tang of orange zest, and a slight sweetness, this little number dances on your tongue and doesn't miss a beat. The sweetener is optional, but it makes the orange and ginger really pop. It'll be tempting to add *more* ginger and orange zest, but be careful. As the soup cools, those flavors get stronger and want a solo. Keep them as the backup artists, and let the squash be the star.

butternut bliss

SERVES 8 AS A STARTER, 6 AS A MAIN

1 tablespoon olive oil or grapeseed oil

1 clove garlic, minced

2 cups (300g) diced yellow onion

Natural salt (see box, page 38) and freshly ground black pepper

1/2 cup (66g) diced celery (about 2 ribs)

1/2 cup (80g) diced carrot (about 1 carrot)

2 cups (280g) cubed orange-flesh sweet potatoes (1-inch/2.5cm cubes)

1 large butternut squash or pumpkin, about 2.5 pounds (1.15 kg), peeled, seeded, and cut into 1-inch (2.5cm) cubes

2 teaspoons minced ginger

8 cups (1.9l) vegetable broth (see page 115)

1/4 teaspoon finely grated orange zest

Pure maple syrup (optional)

In a large saucepan, heat the oil over medium heat. Add the garlic, onion, and 1/4 teaspoon each of salt and pepper. Sauté for 5 minutes, until the onion is soft and translucent. Add the celery and saute for 5 minutes, then stir in the carrot, sweet potatoes, butternut squash, and ginger. Add the vegetable broth and 1/4 teaspoon of salt. Increase the heat to high and bring just to a boil, then reduce the heat to medium and simmer gently for 30 minutes, until the vegetables are completely tender. Remove the saucepan from the heat and stir in the orange zest.

Allow the soup to cool slightly, then pour it into your blender in batches and puree on high for 1 to 2 minutes, until smooth and creamy. (Remember to remove the plastic cap in the blender top and cover the opening with a kitchen towel so steam can escape while you blend.) Return the soup to the saucepan and warm over low heat. Add maple syrup to taste and serve.

s'blended soups

Soup is the ultimate nutritious comfort food. Broth, herbs, seasonings, and raw, roasted, or baked vegetables can create a tasty, impressive dish with no fuss and little expense. Soup is a great way to use up veggies on their last legs, and it typically freezes well. Here are my top tips for creating showstopping soups on the fly.

begin with the broth

Not all broths are created equal. Many boxed and canned broths, which are either under- or oversalted, can be bland or overpowering. Some are just MSG-assisted swill. Your broth can be a major element of taste, even if the soup has an assertive flavor base, so its quality is mission-critical. At the same time, you want the flavors of the veggies to shine, not be overwhelmed by a bully broth that muscles in for star billing. After homemade broth (see page 115), I favor vegetable stock cubes rather than prepared liquids. Cubes let me control the strength of flavor and quantity of broth I prepare. A single cube (or a portion of one) can also add a rich finish to soups, curries, stews, and sauces.

the dream team

I start many soups with a base of chopped red or yellow onion (or leeks, shallots, or green onions) and raw or roasted garlic, sautéed in a bit of oil. I use olive, grapeseed, or, where flavor appropriate, coconut oil. For a more intense flavor, I caramelize the onions and the garlic. I decide on the right amount of garlic and onion by considering the flavors of my other ingredients. Tomato (see Rich but Simple Tomato, page 106) can handle a lot, whereas cauliflower (see Creamy Cauliflower, page 104) benefits from less. High-water-content vegetables like zucchini (green or yellow) added to a base of cooked garlic and onion enhance body and texture without overpowering the star ingredients. To my bases, I add one pinch to $1/8$ teaspoon of salt and sometimes freshly ground pepper to bring out the natural sweetness in the vegetables.

season in stages

How much salt to add is a matter of personal preference, your specific health guidelines, and how salty your broth is. I season gradually, in pinches, tasting until I get the most well-rounded flavor. Salting only once, after everything is cooked, can deliver a salty flavor on the front end and leave the rest of the taste flat. I salt the base, and then check after adding the featured vegetables, and again halfway through simmering. Resist the urge to be heavy-handed, as saltiness can intensify with cooking. I recommend cooling the soup slightly before the final salt check, just before serving. As high temperature can mute our sense of taste, a steaming hot soup crying out for salt may be perfect once slightly cooled. (For the skinny on salt, see page 37.)

layer flavors, roast, and can

Add vegetables in stages. After onion, garlic, and zucchini (or other mild additions to the base), add root vegetables like carrots and parsnips, tubers like potatoes, starchy vegetables like butternut squash, and then cauliflower. About five minutes before the end of simmering, add non-leafy green vegetables like broccoli, beans, and peas. And then finally, add the leafy greens, for which my mnemonic is "leafy means last." You'll get the best results with kale, spinach, and chard if you barely wilt them by adding in the final minutes of simmering. This ensures that the greens don't overcook and they retain their vibrant color (see Dream of Spinach, page 108).

Pre-roasting keynote players like tomatoes, bell peppers, sweet potatoes, yams, pumpkin, butternut squash, carrots, brussels sprouts, broccoli, cauliflower, and beets makes them even more flavorful additions to a soup. To keep the soups in this book quick and easy, I've not called for any pre-roasting, but if you're up for the added step, it will give your pot more personality.

Certain fresh vegetables can get a boost by adding canned or dried versions of the same. Consider tomatoes: the quality of fresh ones varies greatly, so combining fresh or pre-roasted with either canned, tomato paste, or sun-dried gives a soup depth (see Rich but Simple Tomato, page 106). Artichokes and bell peppers can also benefit from this strategy.

slow and low

A slow and steady simmer will gently guide your vegetables to perfection. This way the steam boils off gently and the soup reduces.

herbs and spice are a good vice

Dried herbs are convenient, but nothing beats the aromatic quality of fresh herbs. A bit of parsley, a sprig of thyme, or a bay leaf adds dimension to a soup (see Thyme for Corn Chowder, page 123). More assertive herbs like rosemary, oregano, sage, marjoram, chives, mint, basil, and dill bring specific personalities to the mix. With herbs, a little goes a long way unless you're looking for an accent flavor, as with pistou (see page 118).

With spices, start with a pinch and build up as flavors develop. Too much spice can irreparably throw off the flavor balance. A light hand is crucial with bold acts like cumin and coriander. Spices bring distinctive character— a pinch or two of cayenne delivers a warm tone with back-end kick and nutmeg can be a spectacular addition to root vegetables, squash, and cauliflower.

Keep it simple. Pick a couple of herbs and spices and let them shine. When in doubt, go with classic combinations. Basil pairs beautifully with tomatoes and bell peppers, thyme is sensational with mushrooms, and rosemary transforms otherwise mundane potatoes and beans.

boost and blast

A dollop of salsa, sun-dried tomato paste, pesto (especially good with hearty vegetable soups), tapenade, miso, roasted garlic, harissa, and other pastes can turn a bland bowl of soup into a taste sensation. You can add these elements at almost any stage—in the pot, in the blender, or at the table.

sweeten the pot

Some blends with naturally sweet vegetables such as tomatoes, corn, butternut squash, and carrots may benefit from a splash of sweetener during cooking and right before serving. With these vegetables, I love to add maple syrup, coconut sugar, or coconut nectar (see Butternut Bliss, page 111). A splash of wheat-free tamari helps pull flavors together, too (see Mushroom Magic, page 107).

cream dream

Raw cashews, macadamias, and blanched almonds add rich creaminess to blended soups. Blending one-quarter cup of soaked nuts (any more can be overwhelming; see page 22 for soaking instructions) into a full batch of cooked soup gives a velvety texture that'll have you swearing there's dairy! Whole almonds don't work as well as blanched because the skins leave a rustic texture, even with high-speed blenders. Milks don't add much creaminess and just make a soup watery. The exception is coconut milk, but go easy—even a small amount encroaches on other flavors. Blending a bit of tofu into broth adds a rich texture. Cauliflower is a brilliant choice, too. Potato is good but easily produces a starchy-waxy mouthfeel that is not always appealing.

lift with lemon

Brighten soups with a teaspoon or tablespoon of lemon juice added right before serving. Lemon works well with potatoes, spinach, broccoli, and most blends that have a bold, green component. Add the lemon juice after the soup cools somewhat so as not to overdo it and wind up with citrus soup. If you plan to freeze leftovers, it's better not to add lemon juice to the whole pot. Instead, put lemon on the table so people can add it to taste. Lime is fabulous for blends with avocado and for spicy soups, both hot and cold, like Asian classics and gazpacho (see page 120). If you're not feeling the citrus love, a splash of apple cider, red wine, or rice vinegar can lift hearty broths, bean stews, and soups containing chard or spinach.

call the grain ball

As an alternative to bread, serve blended savory soups topped with a scoop (I use an ice cream scoop) of cooked grain like quinoa, millet, buckwheat, amaranth, or brown rice. Day-old reheated grain is best because it holds together in a ball. Garnished with chopped fresh herbs, this addition contributes to a beautiful presentation and makes a bowl a meal.

freeze then please

Most soup freezes well. Blended soups can develop a lumpy consistency or separate (particularly if you've used nuts) while defrosting. If this happens, just throw the soup back into the blender to restore it to full glory.

taking stock of the situation

Making vegetable broth is a fabulous way to use random vegetables cluttering up the bottom drawer of your fridge. A basic one can be made in 2 to 3 hours, and you don't have to stand over the stove for much of that time.

My stock base usually includes:

> 2 white or yellow onions (green onions, shallots, or leeks work, too)
>
> 2 or 3 cloves garlic
>
> 1 or 2 ribs celery
>
> 2 carrots
>
> $1/2$ bunch flat-leaf parsley
>
> A few sprigs of thyme
>
> 1 or 2 bay leaves, or a 1-inch (2.5cm) piece of kombu seaweed, which adds minerals

To that, I add whatever veggies tickle my fancy (in addition to the ones listed here, I also use potatoes, parsnips, turnips, and tomatoes):

> A handful of shredded green cabbage
>
> 1 broccoli stalk (not the florets)
>
> 1 dozen green beans
>
> A fennel bulb, or a couple of handfuls of mushrooms
>
> Natural salt and freshly ground black pepper
>
> A splash of wheat-free tamari or soy sauce (optional)

To prepare the stock, rough-chop the veggies, throw them in a pot, cover with water, and bring to a boil over high heat. Reduce the heat to the lowest setting that will keep the stock just simmering for a couple of hours. Season to taste; remember, you'll likely salt whatever you make with the broth, too. Allow the broth to cool, and then strain it through a fine-mesh sieve. The stock will keep in an airtight container in the fridge for up to a week, or in the freezer for about 3 months.

note: If you don't have time for homemade vegetable stock, I favor Massel brand stock cubes (see Resources, page 209), which have a mild, well-rounded flavor. They're also vegan, gluten-free, lactose-free, kosher, and contain no MSG. One stock cube for every 2 cups of water yields a broth suitable for most vegetable soups.

This delicious blend of alkalizing vegetables is *souper* healthy and satisfying. The cauliflower and blanched almonds create a rich, creamy texture and the hint of lemon juice brightens the flavors to let the asparagus shine. The lemon intensifies as the soup cools, so add the juice to individual portions just before serving to get the most balanced flavor profile.

alkalizing asparagus

SERVES 6 AS A STARTER, 4 AS A MAIN

2 tablespoons olive oil

2 teaspoons minced garlic (about 2 cloves)

2 cups (200g) chopped leeks (white parts, from 2 or 3 leeks)

Natural salt (see box, page 38)

1/4 cup (33g) diced celery (about 1 rib)

1 cup (135g) diced green zucchini (about 1 medium)

1 cup (135g) diced long yellow squash (about 1 medium)

1 cup (120g) chopped cauliflower florets

7 cups (1.65l) vegetable broth (see page 115)

6 cups (750g) chopped asparagus (1/2-inch/1cm pieces)

1/4 cup (12g) finely chopped flat-leaf parsley

1/4 cup (35g) blanched slivered raw almonds, soaked (see page 22)

1 teaspoon freshly squeezed lemon juice

Heat the oil in a large saucepan over medium heat. Add the garlic, leeks, and 1/4 teaspoon of salt and sauté for 3 to 4 minutes, until the leeks are translucent. Add the celery and saute for 2 minutes. Stir in the zucchini, squash, and the cauliflower and sauté for 2 minutes more. Add the vegetable broth, increase the heat to high, and bring just to a boil. Reduce the heat to medium and simmer, uncovered, for 10 minutes, until the cauliflower is al dente. Add the asparagus and parsley and simmer for 5 to 10 minutes more, until the asparagus is tender but still crisp. (What is worse than overcooked asparagus?)

Remove the saucepan from the heat and allow the soup to cool somewhat; stir in the almonds. Pour the soup into your blender in batches and puree on high for 1 to 2 minutes, until smooth and creamy. (Remember to remove the plastic cap in the blender top and cover the opening with a kitchen towel so steam can escape while you blend.)

Return the soup to the saucepan, add salt to taste, and warm it over medium-low heat.

To serve, ladle the soup into bowls and stir a little lemon juice into each to bring out the flavors.

variation: If you're not a huge fan of asparagus but still want to get in on the pH power, double the amount of cauliflower. This variation transforms the blend into a hearty vegetable soup that is equally tasty but not as asparagus focused.

If you're into chilled soups, it's pretty hard to beat this one. Ready in about ten minutes, this chilled blend has a complex flavor that is rich and inviting without being heavy, and has been known to convert people who are ardently opposed to the cold side. Incredibly alkalizing, this soup delivers on flavor *and* pH promise. Devour it from bowls, or share the love by serving it in shot glasses at a party.

chilled avo and cuke

SERVES 4 AS A MAIN, 32 IN SHOT GLASSES FOR A PARTY

1 1/2 cups (360ml) water

3 cups (435g) peeled, seeded, and diced cucumber, plus more to garnish

2 avocados, pitted, peeled, and chopped, plus 1 avocado, pitted, peeled, and sliced, to garnish

1/4 cup (7g) firmly packed arugula

1/4 cup (7g) finely chopped cilantro, plus more to garnish

3 1/2 tablespoons freshly squeezed lime juice

2 tablespoons cold-pressed extra-virgin olive oil

1 tablespoon finely chopped green onion (white and green parts)

2 teaspoons minced garlic (about 2 cloves)

1/2 teaspoon finely chopped serrano chile, plus more to taste

1 teaspoon natural salt (see box, page 38), plus more to taste

Throw all of the ingredients into your blender and puree on high for 1 to 2 minutes, until smooth and creamy. Tweak chile to taste. Transfer the soup to a bowl, cover, and chill in the fridge for 2 hours.

Remove from the fridge and salt to taste. Serve each bowl of soup garnished with a fan of sliced avocado, a bit of diced cucumber, and a sprinkle of cilantro. (If you're serving the soup in shot glasses, skip the avocado garnish or cut the slices into tiny pieces.)

No, not all of my soups are blended! This chunky dish is a prime example of how a basic *pistou* (as the French call it) can take simple to spectacular. It's my partner, Scott's, favorite meal, so to keep things interesting, I vary the vegetable-and-bean blend, the pistou, or both. (Sundried tomato and macadamia pistou is delightful.) This soup freezes well if you freeze the soup and pistou separately and without the additional lemon juice. You can easily make pistou in a food processor, but I use a blender because it provides smooth texture with no chunky bits.

I keep the flavors of the soup itself pretty mild so the pistou really shines. The pistou tastes great without the miso if you can't find it, but this addition gives it a rich and cheesy taste that is downright incredible. Once you stir the pistou into your soup, you'll be transported. The soup and pistou are meant to be served together, but for people who don't like pistou, I omit it, increase the quantity of herbs and seasonings in the soup, and add a bit more pasta.

white bean and vegetable with pistou

SERVES 8 AS A STARTER, 6 AS A MAIN; THE PISTOU MAKES 1³/₄ CUPS (420G)

soup

2 tablespoons olive oil

2 cloves garlic, minced

1 yellow onion, diced

Natural salt (see box, page 38) and freshly ground black pepper

2 ribs celery, diced

1 carrot, diced

2 red-skinned potatoes, peeled and diced

2 teaspoons finely chopped rosemary

2 teaspoons finely chopped thyme

1 zucchini, diced

1 cup (125g) cut green beans (1-inch/2.5cm pieces)

10 cups (2.4l) vegetable broth (see page 115)

1 (15-ounce/425g) can chickpeas, drained and rinsed well

1 (15-ounce/425g) can cannellini beans, drained and rinsed well

¹/₂ cup (50g) gluten-free or regular shell pasta

¹/₂ cup (25g) finely chopped flat-leaf parsley

¹/₂ cup (40g) finely chopped green onion (white and green parts)

pistou

¹/₃ cup (80ml) cold-pressed extra-virgin olive oil

2 cups (340g) fresh or frozen green peas

¹/₂ cup (70g) sliced or blanched slivered raw almonds or toasted pine nuts

1 teaspoon minced garlic (about 1 clove)

1 tablespoon plus 2 teaspoons freshly squeezed lemon juice

1 teaspoon natural salt, plus more to taste

¹/₄ teaspoon freshly ground black pepper

2 tablespoons finely chopped flat-leaf parsley

¹/₈ teaspoon finely grated lemon zest (optional)

1 teaspoon white miso paste (optional, but it makes the pistou incredible)

1 or 2 lemons, cut into wedges and seeded

To make the soup, heat the oil in a large saucepan over medium heat. Add the garlic, onion, $1/4$ teaspoon of salt, and $1/8$ teaspoon of pepper and sauté for about 5 minutes, until the onion is soft and translucent. Stir in the celery, carrot, and potatoes and sauté for 5 minutes more. Stir in the rosemary and thyme. Add the zucchini, green beans, broth, chickpeas, cannellini beans, and pasta. Increase the heat to high, bring the soup to a boil, and cook for 5 minutes. Lower the heat to medium-high and cook at a lively simmer for 10 to 15 minutes more, until the pasta is al dente. Reduce the heat to medium-low, add the parsley and green onions, and simmer slowly for 5 minutes more. Season to taste with salt and pepper.

To make the pistou, throw all of the ingredients into your blender and blast on high for 30 to 60 seconds, until smooth and well combined. Tweak flavors to taste (you might want more salt).

To serve, put a couple of tablespoons of pistou on the bottom of each bowl and ladle the soup over the top. Pass the lemon wedges and the remaining pistou at the table.

The name says it all. Gazpacho rocks, and this concoction delivers a surprising taste explosion with every spoonful. A happy blend of sweet and spicy, the flavors in this chilled first course or main mellow nicely with time. In fact, the change in flavor is quite pronounced. This is particularly true of the onion. Like a fabulous sangria (see page 174), this soup is better the next day. But, it's delicious a few hours after preparing, so don't feel like you have to wait beyond the three-hour chill.

watermelon gazpacho is the bomb!

SERVES 8 AS A STARTER, 6 AS A MAIN

4 cups (640g) roughly chopped seedless watermelon, plus 6 cups (960g) diced

2 cups (300g) diced tomato

1 cup (145g) peeled, seeded, and diced cucumber

$1/2$ cup (70g) diced red bell pepper

2 tablespoons diced red onion, plus more to taste

3 tablespoons finely chopped basil

3 tablespoons finely chopped mint

3 tablespoons freshly squeezed lime juice, plus more to taste

1 teaspoon finely grated lime zest

2 teaspoons minced ginger

$1/2$ teaspoon minced green serrano chile, plus more to taste

$1/2$ tablespoon natural salt (see box, page 38), plus more to taste

Pinch of freshly ground black pepper

Put the 4 cups of chopped watermelon into your blender and puree on high for 30 to 60 seconds, until liquefied. Pour into a serving bowl. Add the 6 cups of diced watermelon and all the remaining ingredients. Stir to combine well. Tweak flavors to taste (you may want more onion, lime juice, chile, or salt).

Cover and chill in the fridge for at least 3 hours, but preferably 12 to 24 hours to allow the flavors to fuse and the vibrant red color to develop. Before serving, tweak flavors again (if it's too spicy, add some lime juice). Pass additional lime juice and salt at the table.

I should have called this recipe "It's Time for Thyme in Corn Chowder!" That herb, along with the parsley, is really delicious in this creamy blend. Oh, I could break into song. I don't have the sage and rosemary, but you get the drift. Since corn is difficult to digest, I rarely eat it. When I do, it's in this soup. I go out of my way to source non-GMO corn, and combine it with alkaline components to balance the high sugar content and acidity (see page 35). This is pure comfort food.

thyme for corn chowder

SERVES 8 AS A STARTER, 6 AS A MAIN

2 tablespoons olive oil or grapeseed oil

2 cloves garlic, minced

1 yellow onion, finely chopped

Natural salt (see box, page 38) and freshly ground black pepper

2 ribs celery, diced

2 carrots, diced

1 red bell pepper, seeded and diced

2 red-skinned potatoes, peeled and diced

6 cups (1.1kg) corn kernels (fresh from 8 to 10 ears, or defrosted frozen)

1 cup (50g) finely chopped flat-leaf parsley

1 tablespoon plus 1 teaspoon finely chopped thyme

5 cups (1.2l) vegetable broth (see page 115), plus more as needed

1 cup (240ml) canned coconut milk (shake, then pour)

Heat the oil in a large saucepan over medium heat. Add the garlic, onion, $1/4$ teaspoon of salt, and $1/8$ teaspoon of pepper and saute for about 5 minutes, until the onion is soft and translucent. Stir in the celery, carrots, bell pepper, and potatoes and sauté for 5 minutes more. Add the corn, half of the parsley, and 1 tablespoon of the thyme. Pour in just enough broth to cover the vegetables, increase the heat to high, and bring the soup just to a boil. Reduce the heat to medium and stir in the coconut milk and salt to taste. Simmer for about 25 minutes, until the vegetables are tender. Remove from the heat and allow the soup to cool slightly. Transfer about 2 cups of the soup into your blender and blast on high for 30 to 60 seconds, until creamy. (Remember to remove the plastic cap in the blender top and cover the opening with a kitchen towel so steam can escape while you blend.) Return the blended mixture to the rest of the soup in the saucepan, stir to combine well, and set over low heat to warm. Add the remaining $1/2$ cup (25g) parsley and 1 teaspoon of thyme. Season to taste with salt and pepper and serve.

the main event

the world is not right without pizza

SERVES 4 TO 8 AS A STARTER, 2 AS A MAIN

2 prepared thin gluten-free or regular pizza crusts (8 to 10 inches/20 to 25cm each)

Olive oil

2 cups (300g) diced yellow onion (about 1 onion)

Natural salt (see page 38) and freshly ground black pepper

2 Yukon Gold (or similar) potatoes, washed, peeled, and sliced very thin

1 teaspoon chopped fresh rosemary (not dried)

2 cups (44g) loosely packed arugula

sauce

1/2 cup (120ml) olive oil

1/4 cup (60ml) balsamic vinegar

1 tablespoon chopped fresh rosemary

1 teaspoon chopped garlic (about 1 clove)

1/4 teaspoon natural salt

Pinch of freshly ground pepper

Prebake the pizza crusts according to the package instructions. Remove the crusts from the oven and set them on lightly oiled baking sheets; turn the oven temperature to 450°F/220°C. (If your pizza crusts don't require prebaking, preheat the oven as above or to the temperature specified on the package.)

Heat 2 tablespoons of oil in a sauté pan over medium heat. Add the onion and a pinch of salt and pepper and sauté for 10 to 15 minutes, until the onion is caramelized. Set aside.

Place the potatoes in a mixing bowl and using your hands, toss the slices with 1/2 teaspoon of olive oil and a pinch of salt and pepper. (This prevents the potatoes from curling up on the pizza while baking.) Set aside.

To make the sauce, throw all of the ingredients into your blender and blast on high for 30 to 60 seconds, until the oil and vinegar are emulsified.

To assemble the pizzas, spread 1 to 1 1/2 tablespoons of the sauce on each crust. Layer on the onions and then the potatoes (on round crusts, I arrange the potatoes in a circle with a small end slice in the middle). Sprinkle 1/2 teaspoon of rosemary over the top of the potatoes on each pizza.

Bake the pizzas until the potatoes are cooked through and browned, about 20 minutes. Remove from the oven and allow the pizzas to cool slightly. Just before serving, drizzle 1 to 2 table-spoons (or more) of the sauce over each pizza. Toss the arugula with 1/2 teaspoon of olive oil and mound 1 cup of leaves on top of each pizza to cover the potatoes. Pass the remaining sauce at the table.

To get my pizza fix, I build flavor with shaved vegetables, herbs, and rich sauces. My friend Stace and I hit the jackpot when we cooked up this little number. "Wow!" we exclaimed, our mouths dripping with balsamic sauce.

I've gone with a pre-made crust so this pizza can be ready in thirty minutes. But a homemade dough is great, too. Blending the sauce on high speed emulsifies it so your pizza won't get oily. The extra sauce is delicious for dipping pizza slices or steamed veggies.

Who doesn't love good pesto (see photo, pages 124–5)? Unfortunately, vegan recipes (which lack the tangy notes of parmesan) often fall short and taste a bit flat. Not anymore. What's the secret? Protein-rich miso. If you don't have a tub of this paste in your fridge, buy one and start using it immediately. This magical ingredient (I favor the unpasteurized white and yellow varieties made with rice and chickpeas) is transformative, and I use it to boost the flavor of many of my recipes. This simple dish can be prepared in just twenty minutes. If you don't have a high-speed blender, you can easily make this pesto in a food processor. I've also included a raw "noodles" option using zucchini, which makes this dish an enzyme energizer. Either way, this is the ultimate quick meal.

pesto pronto

SERVES 4

1 pound (450g) gluten-free or regular pasta (or 4 zucchini, spiralized to make raw "noodles"; see note, below)

1 cup (150g) halved cherry tomatoes (optional)

pesto

1/3 cup (80ml) cold-pressed extra-virgin olive oil, plus more to taste

3 cups (75g) loosely packed basil

1/2 cup (70g) raw or toasted pine nuts

2 cloves garlic, plus more to taste

2 tablespoons freshly squeezed lemon juice, plus more to taste

1 teaspoon white or yellow miso paste (see Resources, page 208)

Pinch of red pepper flakes, plus more to taste (optional)

1/4 teaspoon natural salt (see box, page 38), plus more to taste

Freshly ground black pepper

1 avocado, pitted and peeled

Put a large pot of salted water over high heat and bring to a boil. Add the pasta and cook according to the package instructions. When the pasta is done to your liking, drain it well and set it aside in a serving dish.

While the pasta is cooking, make the pesto. Throw the olive oil, basil, pine nuts, garlic, lemon juice, miso, pepper flakes, and salt into your blender. Blast on high for 30 to 60 seconds, until well combined. Season with black pepper and tweak the flavors to taste (you may want more garlic, lemon juice, pepper flakes, or salt).

Pour the pesto into a bowl and mash in the avocado. Work quickly so the avocado retains its color. Add the pesto to the pasta and toss well. Dribble in additional olive oil and toss, until you get your desired consistency. Serve the pasta right away, topped with the cherry tomatoes.

vegetable spiralizer

This inexpensive, easy-to-use machine turns vegetables into long, noodle-like strands to make gluten-free raw "pasta."

A big bowl of chili is pure soul food, and this blend is loaded with vegetables and warming spices. It's always a crowd pleaser, and so easy to make. The amount of heat you get depends on the type of chili powder you use. With powerful and exotic spices, this could be alarmingly spicy. But my recipe is mild, with a delightful sweetness. Don't feel locked into using the beans I call for, either. This is just the combination I favor.

if you're chilly grab some chili

SERVES 6 TO 8

2 (14.5-ounce/411g) cans unsalted whole or diced tomatoes (not crushed)

2 tablespoons tomato paste

2 cups (480ml) vegetable broth (see page 115)

2 tablespoons olive oil

1 tablespoon minced garlic (3 or 4 cloves)

2 cups (300g) finely chopped onion (about 1 large onion)

1/2 cup (66g) diced celery (about 2 ribs)

1 cup (160g) diced carrot (about 1 carrot)

1/2 cup (70g) diced red bell pepper

1/2 cup (70g) diced yellow or orange bell pepper

2 teaspoons natural salt (see box, page 38)

1 teaspoon dried oregano

2 teaspoons ground cumin

1 teaspoon smoked paprika

3 tablespoons chili powder

1/8 teaspoon cayenne pepper

1/2 teaspoon freshly ground black pepper

1 cup (90g) diced baby bella or cremini mushrooms

1/2 cup (68g) diced zucchini

2 cups (300g) diced tomato

1 (15-ounce/425g) can red kidney beans, drained and rinsed thoroughly

1 (15-ounce/425g) can pinto beans, drained and rinsed thoroughly

1 (15-ounce/425g) can great northern or cannellini beans, drained and rinsed thoroughly

1 bay leaf

1 tablespoon freshly squeezed lime juice

1/4 cup (7g) plus 2 tablespoons chopped cilantro

1 avocado, pitted, peeled, and sliced

Place the canned tomatoes and their juices, the tomato paste, and the broth into your blender and pulse a few times on low, until rustically combined. Set aside.

Heat the olive oil in a large saucepan over medium heat. Add the garlic, onion, celery, carrot, bell peppers, and 1 teaspoon of the salt and sauté for about 5 minutes, until the vegetables are soft. Stir in the oregano, cumin, paprika, chili powder, cayenne, and black pepper and sauté for 30 seconds. Throw in the mushrooms and zucchini and stir well. Stir in the blended tomato mixture, tomatoes, beans, bay leaf, and the remaining 1 teaspoon of salt. Bring the chili to a boil, and then reduce the heat to low. Simmer for 30 to 40 minutes, stirring occasionally, until the liquid reduces by about one third.

Remove the chili from the heat and stir in the lime juice and the 1/4 cup (7g) of cilantro. Serve in bowls topped with a couple of avocado slices and a sprinkle of the remaining cilantro.

My friend Stacey demanded I turn the mushroom gravy we made into a main dish. "This isn't an accompaniment," she said, "this is a *star*!" This stroganoff is quick and easy, creamy and delicious without all of the fat. Use a variety of exotic mushrooms to kick this into mind-blowing territory.

creamy mushroom stroganoff

SERVES 4

3 tablespoons olive oil

1/2 cup (75g) diced yellow onion

2 teaspoons minced garlic (about 2 cloves)

6 cups (540g) sliced white button and cremini mushrooms

2 cups (480ml) vegetable broth (see page 115)

12 ounces (345g) firm silken tofu or firm regular tofu

3 tablespoons wheat-free tamari or soy sauce

1 teaspoon chopped thyme (not dried)

1/8 teaspoon freshly ground black pepper, plus more to taste

Natural salt (see box, page 38)

12 ounces (340g) gluten-free or regular fettuccini or spaghetti

1/4 cup (12g) chopped flat-leaf parsley, plus more to garnish

2 tablespoons finely chopped chives

Heat 1 tablespoon of the olive oil in a large saucepan over medium-high heat and sauté the onion for about 5 minutes, until soft and translucent. Reduce the heat to low and add the remaining 2 tablespoons of oil. Throw in the garlic and mushrooms and sauté for about 15 minutes, until the mushrooms are soft. Remove from the heat and set aside.

Put 1 cup (240ml) of the vegetable broth and the tofu into your blender and purée on high for 30 to 60 seconds, until smooth and creamy. Add about 1 cup (180g) of the mushroom mixture. Pulse a few times to break them up. You want a speckled, grainy consistency, not a puree.

Pour the blended tofu-mushroom mixture into the saucepan and stir in the tamari, thyme, and pepper. Bring the mixture just to a boil over high heat; reduce the heat to medium and simmer, stirring often, for about 5 minutes, until the sauce thickens. Increase the heat to high and add 1/2 cup (120ml) of the remaining broth. Bring the sauce just to a boil, reduce the heat to medium-high, and simmer for about 10 minutes, until reduced by half. Increase the heat to high again and add the remaining broth. Bring the sauce just to a boil, and then reduce the heat to medium and simmer for 10 minutes more, until creamy. Cover and keep warm.

Cook the pasta according to the package instructions. Drain the pasta and add it to the mushroom sauce. Add the parsley and stir to combine. Season to taste with salt and pepper and serve family-style in a big bowl garnished with the chives and parsley.

wheat-free tamari and liquid aminos

I often add natural, wheat-free tamari (gluten-free soy sauce) to savory dishes to add saltiness and depth of flavor, and to bring out the natural earthiness in vegetables. Nama shoyu
(unpasteurized soy sauce) can be used in raw recipes. However, it's not gluten-free. An alternative to soy sauce is Bragg liquid aminos. Made from unfermented soybeans and water,
this product is a good source of protein. For those with soy allergies, there's also coconut
aminos, which taste like light soy sauce.

This taco "meat" comes pretty close to the real thing, but it's packed with live enzymes and alkalizing boosters. You can whip up this super-tasty taco feast in less than thirty minutes, and you'll get better results with a food processor than with a conventional blender. For a more traditional taco, use non-GMO corn tortillas in place of or wrapped around the romaine. If you go without the romaine, add a bit of shredded lettuce. After devouring a whole batch of the filling, my friend Denise exclaimed: "I want to be buried with this!"

alkaline tacos

SERVES 8 AS A STARTER, 4 AS A LIGHT LUNCH OR MAIN (MAKES 16 TO 20 TACOS)

filling

1/2 cup (55g) raw walnuts

1/2 cup (70g) blanched slivered raw almonds

1/2 cup (45g) soaked, drained, and roughly chopped sun-dried tomatoes (see page 24)

2 tablespoons cold-pressed extra-virgin olive oil

1 teaspoon ground cumin

1 teaspoon ground coriander

1/8 teaspoon garlic powder

1/8 teaspoon onion powder

1/8 teaspoon chili powder

1 1/2 teaspoons Bragg liquid aminos, wheat-free tamari, or soy sauce, plus more to taste

1/8 teaspoon natural salt (see box, page 38), plus more to taste

1 tablespoon chopped flat-leaf parsley

pico de gallo

1 cup (150g) diced tomato

1 1/2 tablespoons finely chopped cilantro, plus more to taste

1 tablespoon diced red onion, plus more to taste

1 teaspoon cold-pressed extra-virgin olive oil

1 teaspoon freshly squeezed lime juice, plus more to taste

1/4 teaspoon minced garlic, plus more to taste

1/4 teaspoon minced serrano chile, plus more to taste

Natural salt

Pinch of freshly ground black pepper

20 medium and large romaine leaves, or other foldable, not-too-soft leaf lettuce, washed and dried

1 or 2 avocados, pitted, peeled, and sliced, to garnish

Slick Sour Cream (see page 199), to garnish

To make the filling, put the walnuts and almonds into your high-speed blender or food processor and pulse until broken up. Add the sun-dried tomatoes, olive oil, spices, liquid aminos, salt, and parsley and pulse until the tomatoes are well incorporated and the mixture is "red and meaty" looking. Tweak flavors to taste (you may want more liquid aminos and salt) and set aside.

To make the pico de gallo, combine the tomatoes, cilantro, onion, olive oil, lime juice, garlic, chile, 1/4 teaspoon of salt, and the pepper. Tweak flavors to taste (you may like more cilantro, garlic, chile, lime juice, onion, or salt).

To assemble the tacos, scoop about 1 tablespoon (depending on the size of the lettuce leaf) of the taco filling into the groove of the leaf. Add a spoonful of pico de gallo, a couple of avocado slices, and a drizzle of sour cream. Repeat with the remaining leaves.

This vegan variation on traditional pad thai strikes a nice balance between sweet and spicy. I love the tanginess of the quick pickles—a great idea I borrowed from my friend Eda. One day she and I made a batch of this pad thai with our fellow pad thai lover, Nikki. Eda wanted more lime juice, Nikki wanted more sugar, and I wanted more heat. Pad thai is like that; everybody prefers it a different way. As a result, I've kept this recipe quite neutral so you can make whatever tweaks you want.

pad thai is always a good idea

SERVES 2 TO 4

1 (14-ounce/395g) package rice stick noodles

2 tablespoons apple cider vinegar

1 tablespoon coconut sugar

2 small radishes

1 1/2 carrots

2 tablespoons wheat-free tamari or soy sauce, plus more to taste

2 tablespoons toasted sesame oil

2 teaspoons freshly squeezed lime juice, plus more to taste

8 ounces (230g) tempeh, thinly sliced, or very firm tofu, cubed

4 green onions, sliced on the diagonal into 2-inch (5cm) pieces (white and green parts)

2 heads baby bok choy, sliced lengthwise into thin strips

Natural salt (optional; see page 38)

sauce

1/4 cup (60ml) toasted sesame oil

1/4 cup (60ml) plus 3 tablespoons wheat-free tamari or soy sauce

1/4 cup (60ml) plus 3 tablespoons coconut nectar (or other natural liquid sweetener; see page 39)

2 tablespoons freshly squeezed lime juice

1 1/2 teaspoons minced garlic (about 2 cloves)

1/2 teaspoon minced ginger

1 teaspoon red curry paste, plus more to taste

1/8 teaspoon dried red pepper flakes

2 cups (120g) bean sprouts, to garnish

1 cup (140g) roughly chopped raw unsalted cashews, to garnish

Cilantro, to garnish

1 lime, cut into wedges, to garnish

Soak the noodles until al dente according to the instructions on the package. Drain and set aside.

In a small bowl, combine the vinegar and coconut sugar. Quickly grate the radishes and the carrot half and transfer the gratings to a glass bowl. Pour the vinegar and sugar mixture over the gratings, cover the bowl, and place it in the refrigerator.

In a sauté pan over medium-high heat, combine the tamari, sesame oil, and lime juice. Add the tempeh and cook for 3 minutes per side, until golden brown and a bit crispy. Remove the pan from the heat and set aside.

To make the sauce, pour the sesame oil, tamari, coconut nectar, lime juice, garlic, ginger, curry paste, and pepper flakes into your blender and blast on high for about 30 seconds, until well combined. Transfer the sauce to a wok or deep sauté pan and bring it just to a boil over high heat. Cut the remaining carrot into julienne. Reduce the heat to medium, stir in the green onions and carrot and cook for 5 minutes. Add the bok choy and cook for about 1 minute more, until the bok choy is just cooked through. Add the noodles and stir until coated with sauce and heated through, about 2 minutes. Add the tempeh and stir carefully. Remove the radish and carrot pickles from the fridge and drain them. Add to the noodles and toss gently. Tweak flavors to taste (you may want more tamari, curry paste, lime juice, or a little salt).

Serve on individual plates or in a big bowl, family style. Top each portion with some bean sprouts, a sprinkling of cashews, and chopped cilantro. Garnish with a lime wedge.

Bursting with vibrant fresh flavors and gorgeous colors, this dish is a winner on every level. It's so rich and sustaining, you almost feel like you're eating something naughty. You can easily stack this lasagna higher if you end up with surplus ingredients. The tomato sauce will come out a bit better if you use a food processor instead of a conventional blender. If you are following an alkaline diet, replace the miso (which is fermented) with yellow mustard powder. This recipe may appear fiddly and slightly overwhelming, but you really can make it in less than an hour, especially if you convince a friend to help. The work is well worth it. I promise.

live lasagna stacks

SERVES 4

4 large zucchini, preferably 2 green and 2 yellow

4 large tomatoes

8 large basil leaves

2 tablespoons cold-pressed extra-virgin olive oil

2 teaspoons gomasio (see note, page 138) or sesame seeds (optional)

tomato sauce

2 tablespoons cold-pressed extra-virgin olive oil

1 cup (90g) chopped sun-dried tomatoes (drained thoroughly and patted dry if packed in oil)

$1/2$ cup (75g) chopped tomato

$1/4$ cup (7g) loosely packed basil

1 tablespoon chopped red onion

$3/4$ teaspoon chopped garlic (about 1 clove)

$1/4$ teaspoon natural salt (see box, page 38)

$1/8$ teaspoon freshly ground black pepper

Pinch of red pepper flakes, plus more to taste

macadamia cheeze

1 cup (140g) raw unsalted macadamias, soaked (see page 22)

$1^1/2$ tablespoons freshly squeezed lemon or lime juice, plus more to taste

1 teaspoon minced garlic (about 1 clove), plus more to taste

2 teaspoons white miso paste, or 1 teaspoon yellow mustard powder

$1/4$ teaspoon natural salt, plus more to taste

2 tablespoons finely chopped cilantro

pesto

$1/2$ cup (120ml) cold-pressed extra-virgin olive oil

$2^1/2$ tablespoons freshly squeezed lemon juice, plus more to taste

5 cups (125g) loosely packed basil

$1/2$ cup (11g) loosely packed arugula

$3/4$ cup (90g) blanched raw almonds, raw unsalted macadamias, or raw pine nuts

2 teaspoons white miso paste, plus more to taste

2 teaspoons minced garlic (about 2 cloves), plus more to taste

$3/4$ teaspoon natural salt, plus more to taste

$1/8$ teaspoon freshly ground black pepper, plus more to taste

Remove the ends of the zucchini and, using a wide vegetable peeler or cheese plane, slice each zucchini lengthwise into strips about $1/8$ inch (3mm) thick. You should have about 40 usable slices. (Yellow zucchini have more seeds, so they may give you fewer usable slices.) Reserve the first and last slices and the seedy ones from the middle to use in a smoothie or soup. Set the slices aside.

Cut the tomatoes crosswise into $1/2$-inch (1cm) rounds and lay them on a few layers of paper towel to draw out the liquid.

To make the tomato sauce, place the olive oil, sundried tomatoes, tomato, basil, onion, garlic, salt, pepper, and pepper flakes into your high-speed blender (or food processor) in the order listed. Pulse on low until well combined. Tweak the pepper flakes to taste. If you add more, be sure to blend the sauce again. Set aside.

To make the macadamia cheeze, place the macadamias, $1/2$ cup (120ml) of water, the lemon juice, garlic, miso paste, and salt into your high-speed blender (or food processor) and pulse once on high, then blend on low for 10 to 20 seconds, until well combined and fluffy. If the mixture is dry and grainy and pieces of nuts are visible, add more water, 1 teaspoon at a time, until you have the consistency of thick, dry hummus. Tweak flavors to taste (you may like more garlic, lemon juice, or salt). Transfer the cheeze to a bowl, stir in the cilantro, and set aside. (Note: If you add the cilantro while blending, the cheeze may turn green.)

To make the pesto, place the olive oil, lemon juice, basil, arugula, almonds, miso paste, garlic, salt, and pepper into your high-speed blender (or food processor) in the order listed. Pulse once on high, then blend on low for 10 to 20 seconds, until well combined. Tweak flavors to taste (you may want more lemon juice, miso, garlic, salt, or pepper).

To assemble the lasagna, lay 3 slices of green zucchini side by side on each of four plates to make a base. Using a spatula or the dull edge of a knife, spread $1/4$ cup (60ml) of tomato sauce on each base. Lay 3 slices of the yellow zucchini on top of the tomato sauce. (If the yellow zucchini slices are short, layer them to match the shape of the base. Next, spread $1/4$ cup (35g) of the cheeze on top of each stack. Lay 2 tomato slices side by side on top of the cheeze. Top the tomatoes with 3 more slices of green zucchini to make another layer. Spread $1/4$ cup (60g) of pesto over the zucchini and top with 2 more slices of tomato. Set 2 basil leaves on top of the tomatoes.

Drizzle $1^{1}/_{2}$ teaspoons of the olive oil over each lasagna and its plate, sprinkle the gomasio on top, and serve.

gomasio

Gomasio is a macrobiotic condiment made from ground, roasted sesame seeds and sea salt. This calcium-rich mix is a fabulous substitute for plain sea salt. It's my go-to finishing touch with main dishes, but it also livens up grains, stir-fries, salads, and steamed veggies. You can purchase prepared gomasio from health food stores or online (see Resources, page 208). To make your own, toast 1 cup of raw sesame seeds in a dry pan until they begin to pop and release a nutty fragrance. Allow the seeds to cool and then combine them with 1$\frac{1}{2}$ tablespoons of natural salt (see box, page 38). Grind everything together with a mortar and pestle or a spice grinder until the seeds are about half crushed. Store in a sealed glass container in the pantry for up to 3 months.

These are my all-time favorite veggie burgers. Hearty and chock-full of complex flavors, these patties are more textured and moist than the store-bought variety. If you have trouble mashing the chickpeas in a conventional blender, simply use a potato masher or food processor and mash with the lemon juice, zest, and broth. Resist the urge to cut back on the spices. The amounts may seem over the top, but the flavors strike a perfect balance when cooked. The combination of vegetables listed here is my favorite accompaniment to these burgers, which makes a complete and elegant meal. However, you could serve these on traditional buns, with a salad, or any other way you like.

spicy chickpea burgers with portobello buns and greens

SERVES 6

burgers

3 tablespoons olive oil

1 cup (150g) diced yellow onion

1 tablespoon finely chopped garlic (about 3 cloves)

1 green serrano chile, seeded, ribbed, and finely chopped

2 tablespoons vegetable broth (see page 115)

2 tablespoons freshly squeezed lemon juice

1 teaspoon finely grated lemon zest

1 1/2 cups (425g) cooked chickpeas (garbanzo beans), or 1 (15-ounce/425g) can, rinsed and drained well

1 1/4 cups (180g) cooked brown rice

1 tablespoon Bragg liquid aminos (see page 132), wheat-free tamari, or soy sauce

1 teaspoon ground cumin

1/2 teaspoon ground coriander

1/4 teaspoon paprika

1/8 teaspoon cayenne pepper

1/2 teaspoon natural salt (see box, page 38)

1/2 cup (15g) finely chopped cilantro

1/2 cup (70g) chickpea (garbanzo bean) flour

6 large portobello mushrooms, stemmed

Olive oil

24 medium-thin stalks asparagus, ends snapped off

24 small cherry tomatoes

Natural salt and freshly ground black pepper

1 1/2 teaspoons finely chopped garlic (about 1 large clove)

6 cups (260g) firmly packed baby spinach

1 teaspoon Bragg liquid aminos, wheat-free tamari, or soy sauce

3 cups (66g) loosely packed arugula

2 1/2 teaspoons freshly squeezed lemon juice

1 1/2 teaspoons gomasio (see note, opposite page) or sesame seeds

To make the burgers, heat 1 tablespoon of the oil in a sauté pan over medium heat. Add the onion and sauté for about 5 minutes, until soft and translucent. Add the garlic and chile, and sauté for about 5 minutes more, until the onion is cooked and just beginning to brown. Remove the pan from the heat and set aside.

continued

spicy chickpea burgers with portobello buns and greens, continued

Pour the broth, lemon juice, and zest into your blender. Add the chickpeas and pulse until combined but still a bit chunky. You may need to stop the machine and scrape down the sides of the container. Using a spatula, transfer the chickpeas to a large mixing bowl, being sure to scrape out every last bit from the blender. Fold in the brown rice and the onion mixture, and then add the liquid aminos, cumin, coriander, paprika, cayenne pepper, and salt and stir well to combine. Add the cilantro and the remaining 2 tablespoons of olive oil and stir until the mixture is wet and well combined. Add the chickpea flour slowly, stirring after each addition, until the mixture is well incorporated. Using your hands, scoop up about 1/2 cup (125g) of the mixture and form a round patty roughly 4 inches (10cm) in diameter; repeat with the remaining mixture to form 6 patties. Place the patties on a plate, cover with plastic wrap, and chill in the fridge for at least 1 hour.

Preheat the oven to 450°F (235°C). Set a large pot of water over high heat to boil.

Place the mushrooms in a large baking dish gill-side up and drizzle with 3 tablespoons of olive oil. Bake for 12 minutes, until fork-tender. Reduce the oven to its lowest setting to keep the mushrooms warm.

Fill a bowl with water and some ice cubes. Add the asparagus to the pot of boiling water and blanch for 2 minutes, until tender but still crisp. Quickly transfer the asparagus to the ice water bath to cool. Once it's cooled, drain the asparagus and set it aside.

Heat 2 tablespoons of olive oil in a large frying pan over medium heat until hot but not smoking. Add the burgers and fry for 4 to 5 minutes, until golden brown. Using two spatulas, carefully flip the burgers and fry for 4 to 5 minutes more, until golden brown and cooked through. (You can also flatten the patties to your desired thickness.) Place the burgers in the oven along with the mushrooms to keep warm.

Slice the cherry tomatoes in half (or leave them whole—whatever your prefer). In a small bowl, toss the tomatoes with 1 tablespoon of olive oil and a pinch of salt and pepper. Set side.

In a deep frying pan or wok, heat 2 tablespoons of olive oil over medium heat until hot but not smoking. Add the garlic and sauté for 1 minute, then add the spinach and liquid aminos and saute for 1 minute more, until just wilted but still green and glossy. Remove the pan from the heat and cover to keep warm.

In a large bowl, toss the arugula with 1 1/2 teaspoons of olive oil, 1/2 teaspoon of the lemon juice, and a pinch of salt. In a separate bowl, toss the asparagus with the remaining 2 teaspoons of lemon juice and a pinch of salt.

To serve, mound 1/2 cup (11g) of the arugula in the center of each of six plates. Place a portobello cap on top of the arugula, gill-side up. Mound equal portions of the spinach mixture on top of the mushrooms. Place a burger on top of the spinach, and then arrange the tomatoes and asparagus around the plate. Drizzle each plate with 1/2 teaspoon of olive oil and sprinkle with 1/2 teaspoon gomasio.

I made this dish with my friend Eda, a curry aficionado. Definitely make your own curry paste for this dish; it tastes fresh and alive, and is full of flavors you won't get with a mass-produced paste. Serve this over quinoa or rice, and to cut down on the cooking time, use sweet potato instead of butternut squash or pumpkin. Increase the chard for an additional chlorophyll boost.

penang curry

SERVES 4

curry paste

3 large (20g) dried New Mexico or California red chile pods

1/4 cup (60g) raw almond or cashew butter

1 tablespoon finely chopped garlic (about 3 cloves)

2 tablespoons finely chopped lemongrass

1 tablespoon finely chopped cilantro root, or 2 tablespoons finely chopped cilantro stems

3 tablespoons finely chopped shallots (about 2 shallots)

2 teaspoons finely grated ginger

1 teaspoon ground turmeric

1/2 teaspoon ground cardamom

1/4 teaspoon ground coriander

1/2 teaspoon ground cumin

2 teaspoons freshly squeezed lime juice

1 teaspoon natural salt (see box, page 38)

2 tablespoons grapeseed oil

2 1/2 cups (600ml) canned coconut milk (shake, then pour)

1 tablespoon wheat-free tamari or soy sauce

3 tablespoons coconut sugar

4 cups (570g) diced butternut squash, pumpkin, or orange-flesh sweet potato

12 ounces (340g) extra-firm tofu, cubed

1 bunch green chard, cut into ribbons or roughly chopped, plus more to taste

1 tablespoon freshly squeezed lime juice, plus more to taste

1/2 cup (70g) raw or toasted cashews, to garnish

1/2 cup (14g) Thai or other basil (large leaves chopped; small leaves left whole), to garnish

To make the curry paste, toast the dried chiles by holding them with tongs directly over a low flame for 5 to 10 seconds, or over a hot electric burner for about 60 seconds, until they puff up and pop. Allow the chiles to cool, then chop them into small pieces, discarding the stems. Fill a bowl with 1/2 cup (120ml) of water, add the chiles (and their seeds), and soak for 10 to 15 minutes, until softened. Pour the chiles and their liquid into your blender; add the almond butter, garlic, lemongrass, cilantro, shallots, ginger, spices, lime juice, and salt and blast on high for 1 to 2 minutes, until creamy. Store the paste in an airtight container in the refrigerator until ready to use, or for up to 1 week.

Heat the grapeseed oil briefly in a large saucepan over medium-high heat. Add the curry paste and stir with a wooden spoon for 1 to 2 minutes, until fragrant and just bubbling. Reduce the heat to low and stir in the coconut milk, tamari, and coconut sugar. Add the squash and cook, covered (but stirring occasionally), for 15 minutes. Stir in the tofu and cook for 10 minutes more. Add the chard and stir gently until the greens are wilted and the squash is cooked through, about 5 minutes more. Remove the pan from the heat and add the lime juice, plus more to taste. Serve garnished with the cashews and basil.

My friend Geoffrey is a phenomenal cook. He and I have so much fun together in the kitchen because we get so excited about the wonders of pure, fresh food, and we enjoy similar flavors. We both love making veggie quinoa bowls, but his special blend with an added wow factor (a green chimichurri sauce that blends up in minutes) is the best I've tasted so far. This combination of veggies and grains is earthy and satisfying, even to the most devoted carnivore. However, it does take $1^{1}/_{2}$ hours to make, so if you don't have that much time, make just the chimichurri sauce and use it to transform any bowl of grains or vegetables (even leftovers) into a brilliant quick meal.

cheerful chimichurri bowl

SERVES 4 TO 6

chimichurri sauce

$^{3}/_{4}$ cup (180ml) cold-pressed extra-virgin olive oil

1 cup (50g) finely chopped flat-leaf parsley, plus more to taste

1 cup (30g) finely chopped cilantro, plus more to taste

2 tablespoons finely chopped tarragon, plus more to taste

2 tablespoons finely chopped mint, plus more to taste

1 teaspoon dried oregano, plus more to taste

$^{1}/_{2}$ cup (40g) finely chopped green onions (white and green parts), plus more to taste

4 cloves garlic, plus more to taste

2 tablespoons freshly squeezed lemon juice, plus more to taste

2 tablespoons freshly squeezed lime juice, plus more to taste

1 teaspoon finely grated lime zest, plus more to taste

$^{1}/_{2}$ teaspoon red pepper flakes, plus more to taste

$^{3}/_{4}$ teaspoon natural salt (see box, page 38), plus more to taste

$1^{1}/_{2}$ teaspoons red wine vinegar, plus more to taste

1 small butternut squash (or pumpkin), peeled, seeded, and cut into thick slices

2 large orange-flesh sweet potatoes, cut into large chunks

Olive oil

10 cloves garlic, peeled

Natural salt

Red pepper flakes

$2^{1}/_{2}$ cups (475g) quinoa

4 large portobello mushrooms, stemmed

1 bunch asparagus, ends snapped off

Freshly squeezed lemon juice

2 bunches rainbow (mixed green and red) chard, stalks removed and leaves roughly chopped

2 avocados, pitted, peeled, and thickly sliced

To make the sauce, throw all of the ingredients into your blender and blast on high for 30 to 60 seconds, until well pureed. Tweak any of the flavors to taste to get it just how you want it. Set aside.

Preheat the oven to 400°F (200°C).

In a large bowl, toss the butternut squash and sweet potato with $^{1}/_{2}$ cup of olive oil, 8 cloves of the garlic, $^{1}/_{4}$ teaspoon of salt, and $^{1}/_{4}$ teaspoon of pepper flakes. Place the vegetables in a single layer on a large baking sheet and bake for about 45 minutes, until tender.

In a Dutch oven or an ovenproof pot with a lid, combine the quinoa with 5 cups (1.18l) of water, 1 tablespoon of salt, and 1 tablespoon of olive oil. Bring to a boil over high heat, then reduce the heat to medium and simmer, uncovered, for 5 to 10 minutes, until the water has reduced below the level of the quinoa. Place the lid firmly on the pot, transfer it to the oven, and bake for 30 to 40 minutes, until the quinoa is nice and fluffy.

In a bowl, toss the mushrooms with 1/4 cup of olive oil. In a separate bowl, toss the asparagus with 2 tablespoons of olive oil, 2 tablespoons of lemon juice, and 1/4 teaspoon salt. In a grill pan set over medium-high heat, grill the mushrooms for 10 to 15 minutes, turning occasionally, until tender and cooked through; grill the asparagus for 5 minutes, turning occasionally, until tender but still crisp. Set the mushrooms and asparagus on a plate lined with paper towels to cool. Cut the mushrooms in large, rustic slices.

In a pan over high heat, sauté the chard with 1 tablespoon of olive oil, 1 teaspoon of lemon juice, 1/2 teaspoon of salt, and a pinch of pepper flakes for about 2 minutes, until the chard is just wilted.

To serve, place 1 cup (170g) of quinoa in the bottom of four noodle or soup bowls. Surround the quinoa in each bowl with about 3 slices of squash, 6 to 8 slices of mushroom, 3 slices of sweet potato, and one quarter of the avocado slices. Place a scoop of chard in the center of each bowl, on top of the grain. Divide the asparagus spears among the bowls and drizzle 1/4 cup (60ml) of chimichurri sauce in each bowl. Serve immediately and pass the remaining sauce at the table.

i-love-veggies! bake

SERVES 6 TO 8

sauce

3 tablespoons olive oil

2 cups (300g) diced yellow onion

Natural salt (see box, page 38)

1 tablespoon finely chopped garlic (about 3 cloves)

2 cups (480ml) vegetable broth (see page 115)

1/2 cup (70g) raw unsalted cashews

1 head cauliflower (about 1 3/4 pounds/800g), cut into florets and steamed

1/4 teaspoon freshly ground black pepper

1 tablespoon finely chopped thyme

1 1/2 teaspoons finely chopped rosemary

1/8 teaspoon paprika

Pinch of cayenne pepper

2 teaspoons freshly squeezed lemon juice

veggie bake

1/2 butternut squash (or pumpkin), peeled, seeded, and very thinly sliced

1/4 cup (20g) plus 2 tablespoons finely chopped green onion (white and green parts)

3 tablespoons finely chopped chives

1/4 cup (12g) plus 1 tablespoon finely chopped flat-leaf parsley

3 large potatoes, very thinly sliced

1 pound (450g) green beans, trimmed and cut into 1-inch (2.5cm) pieces

1 large orange-flesh sweet potato, peeled and very thinly sliced

1 cup (90g) sliced almonds

3 tablespoons dried onion flakes

To make the sauce, heat 2 tablespoons of the olive oil in a shallow saucepan over medium heat. Add the onion and a pinch of salt and sauté for about 5 minutes, until the onion is translucent. Add the garlic and sauté for 5 to 10 minutes, until the onion starts to brown. Put the broth, cashews, and onion mixture into your blender and purée on high for 30 to 60 seconds, until smooth and creamy. Add half of the cauliflower and blast on high for about 30 seconds more, until combined. Add the remaining cauliflower, 2 teaspoons of salt, the pepper, thyme, rosemary, paprika, cayenne, and lemon juice and puree for about 1 minute, until smooth and creamy. Set aside.

Preheat the oven to 375°F (190°C) and lightly grease a 3 1/2-quart (3.5l) baking dish with oil.

To make the veggie bake, lay the butternut squash in the bottom of the baking dish in overlapping rows. Add 1 1/4 cups (300ml) of the sauce and sprinkle 2 tablespoons of the green onion, 1 tablespoon of the chives, and 1 tablespoon of the parsley over the top. Layer on the potatoes and cover with 1 1/4 cups (300ml) of the sauce. Sprinkle on 2 tablespoons of the green onion, 1 tablespoon of the chives, and 1 tablespoon of the parsley. Layer on the beans and cover with 1 1/4 cups (300ml) of the sauce. Sprinkle on the remaining green onion, chives, and 1 tablespoon of the parsley. Add the sweet potatoes and cover with the remaining sauce.

Cover with aluminum foil and bake for 1 hour. Uncover and sprinkle the almonds and onion flakes over the top. Bake for about 15 minutes more, until the vegetables are cooked through. Cool for 5 minutes, then serve family-style, sprinkled with the remaining parsley.

This recipe is a commitment; it's the most involved dish in the book, but it also gets raves like "epic" every time I put it on the table. I made the yield extremely generous to make the payoff worth the effort. This dish is absolutely scrumptious and hearty on its own, but you can also add cannellini beans or chickpeas along with the green beans to boost the protein. If you blend in some extra broth with the cauliflower, the sauce makes a spectacular soup.

Pancakes on a Sunday morning is heaven. I like my mine light, just a bit brown and crispy on the edges and with a subtle sweetness. But gluten-free, vegan pancakes can be tricky to make. After trying countless ideas, I got close to perfection, but the batter was still a little too heavy. So I called in reinforcements, contacting my dear friend Ricki, the most talented gluten-free and vegan baker I know. She simply added apple cider vinegar and then called me proclaiming, "You have a *winner*!" My friend Kate and her daughter, Devin, also got excited about this recipe and pioneered a waffle version. I tried it myself and they are equally delicious. Score!

fluffy gf pancakes

MAKES 8 PANCAKES; SERVES 4

1 cup (240ml) unsweetened almond or other milk (strained if homemade)

2 tablespoons coconut oil in liquid form

3 tablespoons pure maple syrup, plus more to serve

2 teaspoons apple cider vinegar

1 tablespoon natural vanilla extract

1³/₄ cups (250g) all-purpose gluten-free flour

¹/₄ cup (31g) tapioca flour

1 teaspoon baking powder

1 teaspoon baking soda

¹/₄ teaspoon natural salt (see box, page 38)

1 tablespoon white or black chia seeds

¹/₂ cup (130g) mashed banana (about 1 banana)

Pure maple syrup (optional)

Grease a frying pan or griddle with a bit of coconut oil and set over medium heat.

Pour the milk, coconut oil, maple syrup, apple cider vinegar, and vanilla into your blender and pulse until smooth. In a large bowl, combine the flours, baking powder, baking soda, salt, and chia seeds with a fork until well combined.

Add the dry ingredients and the banana to the mixture in your blender and pulse on low to medium (in a high-speed blender) or high (in a conventional blender), just until combined. You may have to stop the machine and scrape down the sides of the container. Don't overblend or the chia seeds will make the batter too thick. (This batter does need to be used right away. And if you try to thin it out by adding more liquid, the pancakes will be soggy in the middle.)

Reduce the frying pan heat to medium-low and pour ¹/₃ cup (80ml) of batter onto the frying pan for each pancake. Cook for 4 minutes, then flip the pancakes and cook for 3 minutes more, until browned. These pancakes take longer to cook than conventional pancakes, and you may feel like you should flip them after less than 4 minutes. Resist this urge or they will not cook in the middle. If they start to get too brown, lower the heat even further.

Serve with maple syrup or your favorite toppings.

A mix of live culture and berry seedy intentions is always a recipe for success. This simple breakfast parfait is not only gorgeous in its simple presentation, it's also loaded with beneficial probiotics, live enzymes, nutrient density, and antioxidant power. It's low in natural sugar, too, making it a wonderful alkaline-forming, immune-boosting, and surprisingly filling start to the day.

Sprout your nuts and seeds to activate their nutrient potential (see page 23). These parfaits are highly adaptable. Use whatever fresh berries and raw nuts and seeds you have, and add different yogurts and creams. The cream I use here takes about 8 hours to culture, but you could also use the Alkaline Sugar-Free Cream (page 201) as a quick alternative. To jazz up the cream, blend in some low-sugar fruit to taste, such as strawberry or cranberry, after culturing. Either way, these make gorgeous edible centerpieces at your next brunch or lunch.

berry seedy but cultured breakfast

SERVES 2

cultured cream

2 cups (360g) young Thai coconut meat (see note, page 200)

3 tablespoons coconut water

3 tablespoons coconut water kefir (see page 30), or ½ teaspoon probiotic powder (see note, page 30)

1 tablespoon alcohol-free vanilla extract

1 teaspoon freshly squeezed lemon juice

5 drops alcohol-free liquid stevia (see page 39), plus more to taste

¼ cup (40g) roughly chopped almonds

1 tablespoon shredded unsweetened coconut

1 tablespoon sunflower seeds

1 tablespoon pumpkin seeds

2 teaspoons shelled hemp seeds

2 teaspoons white or black chia seeds

2 teaspoons ground flaxseeds

1 cup (160g) raspberries

½ cup (80g) sliced strawberries (about 4 strawberries)

1 cup (170g) blackberries

To make the cultured cream, put the coconut meat, coconut water, and kefir into your blender and blend on high for 30 to 60 seconds, until smooth and creamy. (If you're using probiotic powder instead of kefir, stir it into the coconut meat and coconut water mixture after blending.) Pour the cream into a glass or ceramic bowl and cover it. Let it stand at room temperature for 8 hours, until fermented and tangy. Once it's ready, stir in the vanilla, lemon juice, and stevia. Tweak stevia to taste.

To assemble the parfaits, in a bowl, combine the almonds, coconut, sunflower seeds, and pumpkin seeds. In a separate bowl, combine the hemp seeds, chia seeds, and flaxseeds. Into each of two (14-ounce/415ml) highball glasses, place the raspberries so they evenly cover the bottom of the glass. Pour the almond-coconut mixture in next and top with half of the cream. Place half of the strawberry slices on top of the cream and sprinkle on the seed mixture. Add the remaining cream and top with the blackberries. Serve immediately, or chill in the fridge for up to 2 hours.

To say I'm addicted to crepes is an understatement. They are just so incredibly versatile. You can fill these crepes with fruit or a hearty savory mix, or even make incredible cannelloni. I'm usually all about substituting whatever you have on hand for my recipes, but in this case, only grapeseed oil works. When pondering a crepe dish to include in the book, I couldn't decide: sweet, savory, or spicy? They all rock, so I decided to include all of them. (I can be greedy like that.) This yummy harmony of notes makes an amazing brunch meal that's dressed to impress.

savory, sweet, and spicy crepes

MAKES 8 CREPES; SERVES 4

batter

2 cups (480ml) unsweetened soy or almond milk (strained if homemade)

1/4 cup (60ml) grapeseed oil

1/2 cup (80g) white rice flour

1/2 cup (80g) chickpea (garbanzo bean) flour

1/2 cup (32g) arrowroot

1/2 teaspoon natural salt (see box, page 38)

filling

4 cups (570g) peeled and diced orange-flesh sweet potato

2 tablespoons olive oil

1 teaspoon red curry paste, plus more to taste

2 teaspoons minced ginger

1 teaspoon minced garlic (about 1 clove)

1 teaspoon ground cinnamon

3/4 teaspoon curry powder, plus more to taste

1/2 teaspoon natural salt

1/8 teaspoon freshly ground black pepper

1/8 teaspoon red pepper flakes, plus more to taste

1/4 cup (38g) coconut sugar

1 1/4 cups (300ml) canned coconut milk (shake, then pour)

1/3 cup (60g) raisins

3/4 cup (120g) roughly chopped raw almonds

1 tablespoon freshly squeezed orange juice

1/4 teaspoon finely grated orange zest

cashew cream

1 cup (140g) raw unsalted cashews, soaked (see page 22)

1/2 cup (120ml) water, plus more as needed

1/4 cup (60ml) freshly squeezed orange juice

2 teaspoons coconut sugar

1/2 teaspoon finely grated orange zest

1/4 teaspoon ground cinnamon, plus more to garnish

1/4 teaspoon finely grated ginger

Pinch of red pepper flakes

1/4 teaspoon natural salt

To make the batter, pour the milk, grapeseed oil, flours, arrowroot, and salt into your blender and blend on medium for 10 to 15 seconds, until well combined with no lumps. You may need to stop the machine and scrape down the sides of the container.

Lightly grease an 8-inch (20cm) nonstick crepe pan or shallow frying pan with grapeseed oil, using a paper towel so the coating is very light. Heat the pan over medium-low heat. Lift the pan off the heat and pour in 1/3 cup (80ml) of the batter, quickly tipping the pan to allow the mixture to swirl and coat the bottom of the pan evenly. Return the pan to the heat and cook for 2 to 3 minutes, until bubbles form on the top and the sides begin to curl away from the pan. Gently flip the crepe with a spatula and cook for 1 to 2 minutes more, until lightly browned. Repeat with the remaining batter, lightly greasing the pan as needed. Stack the finished crepes on top of each other on a plate to soften.

To make the filling, place the sweet potato into a pot fitted with a steamer. Add 1 inch (2.5cm) of water to the pot, set over high heat, and cover. Steam the sweet potato for about 15 minutes, until al dente. Drain the sweet potato well. Heat a wok or a deep frying pan over medium heat. Add the oil, curry paste, ginger, garlic, cinnamon, curry powder, salt, pepper, pepper flakes, and coconut sugar and mix well. Stir in the sweet potato and cook for 1 to 2 minutes, until fragrant, well combined, and just beginning to bubble. Add more curry paste or powder to taste. Stir in the coconut milk, raisins, and almonds and simmer for 8 to 10 minutes, until the liquid has thickened and almost completely reduced, and has a silky consistency. Stir in the orange juice and zest; remove from the heat and set aside.

To make the cashew cream, throw all of the ingredients into your blender and blast on high for 1 to 2 minutes, until smooth and creamy. You may need to add a bit more water to achieve a drizzling consistency.

To serve, spoon some of the sweet potato filling along one side of each crepe. Carefully roll up the crepes, starting from the side with the filling. Top each crepe with a crisscross drizzle of cashew cream and a sprinkle of cinnamon. Serve immediately.

desserts

Hello, my name is Tess, and I'm a chocoholic. Well, a raw, organic, fair-trade cacao addict. It runs in the family. My sister, Kara, has a saying: "A chocolate a day keeps the grouchies away." Based on this theory, a slice of this delectable offering is likely to keep you in a constant state of euphoria. This torte is consistently among the top three raved-about recipes on my site, and a beacon of hope for all of you fellow chocolate addicts who are not inclined to spend more than fifteen minutes preparing your fix. I like to serve this torte with Cashew Cream (page 200), some shavings of raw vegan chocolate, and orange zest. This dessert is decadent and incredibly rich, and a tiny sliver usually satisfies even the most deprived aficionado. So, you may have leftovers. Chocolate for breakfast anyone?

raw chocolate–orange torte

MAKES 20 SATISFYING SLIVERS, 10 TO 12 ADDICT-SIZE SLABS

crust

1 cup (160g) raw whole almonds

1/2 cup (80g) firmly packed chopped pitted dates, plus more as needed

1/4 cup (18g) cacao powder or unsweetened cocoa powder

filling

1 cup (240ml) coconut oil in liquid form

1 cup (240ml) freshly squeezed orange juice

3/4 cup (180ml) raw agave nectar

1/2 cup (35g) cacao powder or unsweetened cocoa powder

3 cups (420g) raw unsalted cashews, soaked (see page 22)

1/4 teaspoon orange extract

Pinch of natural salt (see box, page 38)

1 teaspoon finely grated orange zest

Cashew Cream (page 200), to garnish (optional)

Shaved vegan chocolate, to garnish (optional)

Finely grated orange zest, to garnish (optional)

To make the crust, grease a 9- or 10-inch (23 or 25cm) springform pan with coconut oil. Put the almonds, dates, and cacao powder into your food processor and process until well combined and the mixture forms a dough. Form the dough into a ball; if the dough doesn't hold together, you may need to add more dates and process again. Press the dough into the bottom of the prepared pan and set aside.

To make the filling, put all of the ingredients into your blender in the order listed and blend for 2 to 3 minutes, until rich and creamy. To achieve the smoothest filling, stop the machine periodically and scrape down the sides of the container. Pour the filling into the crust. Cover the pan with aluminum foil and freeze the torte for 8 hours.

To serve, transfer the pan from the freezer to the fridge at least 1 1/2 hours before serving; let the torte defrost in the fridge for about 30 minutes. Remove the sides of the springform pan and then cut the torte into slices with a very sharp knife. Keeping the slices together, return the torte to the fridge to continue defrosting for at least an hour before serving.

note: Because of the coconut oil, this filling will melt if left out at room temperature.

Baked fruit always gets my vote. It's a simple dessert, with a natural, rich sweetness that satisfies. Oh, and where do I profess my undying love for apple pie? These baked caramel apples satisfy my cravings for baked fruit and pie, and I don't even *knead* to grab my rolling pin. Throw some apples in the oven; dress them up in a super-easy, raw caramel sauce (that you would swear is cooked); add a scoop of cream (see page 200); and you've got a fabulous last-minute dessert.

oh, wow! baked caramel apples

SERVES 4

4 large apples

1/4 cup (60ml) water

1/2 cup (55g) chopped raw walnuts or pecans, to garnish

caramel sauce

1/4 cup (60ml) unsweetened almond milk (strained if homemade)

1/2 cup (120ml) plus 1 table-spoon pure maple syrup

1/2 cup (80g) firmly packed chopped pitted dates, soaked (see page 22)

1/3 cup (47g) raw unsalted cashews, soaked (see page 22)

1 teaspoon alcohol-free vanilla extract

1/2 teaspoon natural salt (see box, page 38), plus more to taste

Preheat the oven to 350°F (180°C).

Core the apples, opening them at the stem end but leaving the bottom closed so you can fill the centers with the caramel sauce and nuts. Make four shallow, diagonal cuts on the skin of each apple to allow steam to escape while baking. Place the apples in a baking dish and add the water. Bake for 30 to 40 minutes, until the skins are shriveled and the flesh is soft. Check the apples at 30 minutes to make sure they don't overcook and burst.

While the apples are baking, make the sauce. Throw all of the ingredients into your blender and blast on high for 2 to 3 minutes, until smooth and creamy. You may need to stop the machine periodically and scrape down the sides of the container. Tweak the salt to taste.

Remove the apples from the oven and let them cool slightly before transferring them to serving plates, top-side up. Using a small measuring cup, fill the center of each apple with caramel sauce, allowing the sauce to overflow onto the plate. Place a few additional dollops of the sauce around the plate and garnish with a good sprinkling of walnuts.

My friend Denise says, "Chocolate is like black. It goes with everything." Well, maybe not everything, but one thing's for sure: banana and chocolate are a match made in heaven. My favorite Australian food magazine, *Delicious*, once ran a fabulous banana split recipe featuring blackened whole bananas in their skins split open to make their own boats. This is my healthy homage to that creative idea, and a fast, fun way to serve a banana split.

chocolate-chile banana spilly

SERVES 6

ice cream

1/4 cup (60ml) unsweetened almond milk (strained if homemade), plus more as needed

1/4 cup (60g) raw or roasted cashew butter

1 tablespoon coconut oil in liquid form

1 tablespoon pure maple syrup, coconut sugar, or coconut nectar

1 teaspoon natural vanilla extract

Pinch of natural salt (see box, page 38)

2 cups (285g) frozen banana chunks (about 2 bananas)

1/4 teaspoon red pepper flakes

1 1/2 cups (360ml) Dark Chocolate Sauce (page 204)

6 large bananas (not overripe, fully intact with skins on)

1/3 cup (37g) roughly chopped raw pecans or walnuts, to garnish

To make the ice cream, put the almond milk, cashew butter, coconut oil, maple syrup, vanilla, salt, and frozen banana into your blender in the order listed and blend on high for 30 to 60 seconds, until smooth and creamy. Add up to 1/4 cup (60ml) more almond milk as needed to reach the proper consistency. (If you're using a high-speed blender, you may only need a bit more milk; conventional blenders will require more.) Transfer the mixture to a sealed container and freeze for no more than 2 hours (any longer and it will crystallize). You could also serve the ice cream soft, without freezing, or freeze the mixture in an ice cream maker per the manufacturer's instructions and store it in the freezer overnight to set.

In a small bowl, stir the pepper flakes into the dark chocolate sauce and set aside.

Place the unpeeled bananas in a large sauté pan over medium heat. Cook for 10 to 15 minutes, turning occasionally, until the banana skins have turned black on all sides. Remove the pan from the heat and let the bananas cool slightly before placing them on serving plates.

To serve, slice open the top of each banana to expose the flesh. Drizzle 2 tablespoons (or more to taste) of the chocolate sauce over the bananas and top with 1 tablespoon of nuts. Serve a scoop of ice cream alongside each banana and pass the remaining chocolate sauce at the table.

One of the great virtues (and pitfalls) of raw recipes is that you can sample them at any stage in the process. The challenge with this one is having any ganache left to actually make the truffles. (I could rename this "Shovel-It-Straight-Into-Your-Gob Fudge.") I made a batch of this with my friend Karen, who confessed midway through blending that she isn't really a fan of chocolate. Horrified, I simply handed the blender to her. After one taste, she clutched the container with Gollum-like greed and exclaimed, "Oh . . . now *that's* exciting!".

chocolate truffles

MAKES 30 TRUFFLES

truffles

1/4 cup (60ml) coconut oil in liquid form

1/4 cup (18g) cacao powder, plus more to taste

3/4 cup (180g) raw cashew butter

1/3 cup (80ml) pure maple syrup

1 tablespoon alcohol-free vanilla extract

Pinch of cayenne pepper, plus more to taste

1/8 teaspoon natural salt (see box, page 38)

coating

1/2 cup of any one of the following, or a mix:

Shredded unsweetened coconut

Crushed shelled pistachios

Crushed raw almonds

Finely grated lime or orange zest

Finely chopped dried lavender

Crushed goji berries

Mesquite powder

Maqui powder

Maca powder

1/2 cup (35g) cacao powder mixed with 1 1/2 teaspoons cinnamon, 3/4 teaspoon natural salt, and 1/4 teaspoon cayenne pepper

To make the truffles, put all of the ingredients into your blender in the order listed. Blend on low for a few seconds, then increase the speed to high (this will keep the cacao powder from flying all over the carriage and save you time scraping down the container) and blend for 30 to 60 seconds, until thick and combined. Tweak flavors to taste (you might like more cacao powder or cayenne). Scrape the mixture into a sealable container and freeze it for at least 2 hours to make it easier to roll. (The coconut oil in the mixture melts very quickly.)

Using a teaspoon, scoop the truffle mixture into your hand and quickly roll it into a ball. (Don't let it warm up or it'll get gooey.) Roll the truffles in your desired coating(s) and then place them on a baking sheet or in a container lined with parchment paper. Chill the coated truffles in the fridge for at least 4 hours; remove just before serving.

I fell in love with homemade granita in Sicily. They scoop it out of large metal canisters there, and it is so refreshing on a hot summer day. This mango-chile version serves up a nice balance of sweet and heat.

mango fire and ice

SERVES 6

1 cup (240ml) coconut water

4 cups (640g) fresh or defrosted frozen chopped mango

3 tablespoons freshly squeezed lime juice

2 teaspoons finely grated lime zest, plus more to garnish

$1/4$ teaspoon finely chopped green serrano chile, plus more to taste

Put all of the ingredients into your blender and blast on high for 30 to 60 seconds, until smooth and creamy. Tweak the chile to taste.

Transfer the granita mixture to a 9 by 13-inch (23 by 33cm) baking dish, cover, and freeze for 1 hour. Remove the granita from the freezer and stir it with a fork, mashing up any frozen bits. Cover and freeze it for 2 hours more, until the granita is firm. Using a fork, scrape the granita vigorously to form icy flakes. Serve in glasses garnished with lime zest.

One of the star recipes on my website, this super-easy pudding is zesty and refreshing. You don't need key limes to make it (you get that flavor by combining limes and lemons). If you are a tart-at-heart (like me) and love sharp, tangy notes, you're going to be in heaven. Those of you who like your citrus on the sweeter side may want to add more agave nectar. Either way, this is sub*lime*.

"key lime" pudding

SERVES 4

⅓ cup (80ml) light agave nectar, plus more to taste

½ cup (120ml) freshly squeezed lemon juice

½ cup (120ml) freshly squeezed lime juice

2 ripe avocados, pitted and peeled (see note, below)

2 cups (285g) chopped bananas (about 2 bananas)

1 teaspoon finely grated lemon zest

1 teaspoon finely grated lime zest

Throw all of the ingredients into your blender and puree on high for 1 to 2 minutes, until well combined. You may need to stop your machine and scrape down the sides of the container to ensure everything is incorporated evenly. Tweak the sweetener to taste. Divide the pudding among four serving glasses and chill in the fridge for about 3 hours to thicken. Serve the same day, chilled, to avoid oxidation.

note: This pudding works best with ripe avocados that don't have any brown discolorations. Over-ripe or bruised avocados detract from the taste.

If the world were ending, I might just whip up this decadent treat as my finale. A rice pudding that you don't have to stir for an hour? Now that makes me weak in the knees. Other reasons to swoon over this dessert: the incredible creaminess and the delicate blend of spices that sing in perfect harmony with the apples, raisins, and maple syrup. Oh, my. Show me the way to heaven with a smile on my face.

chai rice pudding

SERVES 6 TO 8

1/4 cup (60ml) plus 3 table-spoons pure maple syrup, plus more to taste

2 tablespoons water

2 apples, peeled, cored, and cubed

1 cup (240ml) canned coconut milk (shake, then pour)

2 teaspoons natural vanilla extract

1/2 teaspoon minced ginger

1 teaspoon ground cinnamon

1/4 teaspoon ground cardamom (see note, opposite page)

1/4 teaspoon ground nutmeg

Pinch of ground cloves

Pinch of natural salt (see box, page 38)

3 cups (450g) cooked short-grain brown rice (soft but not mushy)

1/4 cup (45g) raisins

1 cup (240ml) unsweetened almond milk (strained if homemade)

1/3 cup (40g) chopped raw pistachios

In a saucepan over high heat, bring the 1/4 cup (60ml) of maple syrup and the water to a boil (this should take less than a minute). As soon as the mixture bubbles, reduce the heat to medium-low and stir in the apples. Cook the apples for about 15 minutes, stirring occasionally, until they caramelize lightly and soften slightly but remain mostly firm.

While the apples are cooking, put the coconut milk, the remaining 3 tablespoons of maple syrup, the vanilla, ginger, spices, and salt into your blender and blast on medium-high for about 10 seconds, until combined. Add 1 1/2 cups (225g) of the rice and process on medium-low for a few seconds, until creamy but rustic. (If you're using a high-speed blender, be careful of overdoing it; you don't want a completely smooth blend here, and it can happen quickly. The pudding will be goopy if you overblend. If you're using a conventional blender, your machine will let you know when the mixture is ready; it'll thicken and be difficult to blend.) Add the blended mixture and the raisins to the cooked apples and stir to combine. Stir in 1/2 cup (120ml) of the almond milk and the remaining 1 1/2 cups (225g) of cooked rice. Reduce the heat to low and simmer for about 5 minutes, until the mixture thickens slightly. Stir in the remaining 1/2 cup (120ml) of almond milk and simmer for 5 minutes more, until you have your desired consistency (I take my rice pudding off the heat as soon as the liquid has been absorbed). Tweak the maple syrup to taste.

Serve warm, at room temperature, or even chilled; add 2 tablespoons to 1/4 cup (60ml) milk if you serve it chilled, to soften it up. Sprinkle pistachios on each serving.

cardamom

Ground cardamom can be difficult to find. If you can find only pods, which are more aromatic, smash them with the flat edge of a knife and extract the seeds. Discard the husks or mull them in tea or another beverage. Grind the seeds in a spice grinder or with a mortar and pestle.

Reminiscent of the Creamsicles you may have eaten as a child, these orange and vanilla–flavored ice pops make great after-school snacks or healthy desserts for kids (and adults!). I use soaked dried apricots to add richness and flavor (and fiber), which reduces the amount of sweetener required. Tweak the sweetener according to your taste buds, but keep in mind that the pops won't taste as sweet once they're frozen.

orange dreamsicles

MAKES 10 TO 12 POPS

1 cup (165g) diced dried apricots

1¼ cups (300ml) unsweetened almond or soy milk (strained if homemade)

1½ cups (360ml) freshly squeezed orange juice

1 large orange, peeled and segmented

1½ tablespoons finely grated orange zest

1 teaspoon alcohol-free vanilla extract

3 tablespoons natural sweetener (see page 39), plus more to taste

Pour boiling water over the apricots and let them soak for 30 minutes, until soft and plump. Drain the apricots and throw them into your blender along with the rest of the ingredients. Blast on high for 1 to 2 minutes, until smooth and creamy. Tweak the sweetener to taste. (If you're using a conventional blender, strain the mixture through a fine-mesh sieve to catch any unblended bits of apricot. Use a spoon to push the mixture through the sieve to get every lost drop.)

Pour the mixture into ice-pop molds and place the molds in the freezer for at least 24 hours. (This allows the pops to get creamy all the way through. If you take them out of the freezer early, they will likely be creamy on the top and icy in the middle.) To release the pops from the molds, run the lower part of the molds under hot water for just a moment.

I love a great date, and I'm not referring to the romantic, dinner-and-a-movie variety. I'm talking about a blending love affair that has you spinning with heart-pounding joy at the union between machine and ingredients. If you're not spending time with chia, get acquainted. She's a s'blended companion in a class of her own, transforming the nature of your food and your healthy life. Treat chia gently in this recipe. You don't want this spoon pudding to be completely blended or it will look like a cross between swamp water and porridge. Dance gracefully with chia, invite orange blossom to join, and you might just fall in love.

a date with chia

SERVES 6

3 cups (720ml) unsweetened almond milk (strained if homemade)

3 tablespoons pure maple syrup, plus more to taste

2 tablespoons alcohol-free vanilla extract

1 teaspoon pure orange-blossom or orange-flower water (see note, below)

1 cup (180g) firmly packed chopped pitted dates

1/2 cup (80g) white or black chia seeds

Grated zest of 1 orange

Pour the almond milk, maple syrup, vanilla, and orange-blossom water into your blender and blend on high for 10 to 20 seconds, until well combined. Add the dates and blast on high until the dates are finely chopped, but not completely blended. (Those of you with high-speed blenders will need to be careful to not overblend.) Add the chia seeds and blend on high for just a few seconds (if you're using a high-speed blender) or 10 to 20 seconds (if you're using a conventional blender), until the chia seeds are incorporated into the mixture but not fully crushed. Pour the mixture into a glass bowl and use a spatula to disperse the chia seeds evenly. Cover and chill in the fridge for 2 to 3 hours, until thickened. (The pudding doesn't set completely.)

Garnish each serving with grated orange zest.

note: You can purchase orange-blossom or orange-flower water from Middle Eastern grocers or specialty stores for just a few dollars. Cortas, the brand I use, is made from the blossoms of bitter orange and is widely available around the world.

When I eat chocolate, I go over to the dark side—and by that I mean the place where rich, raw, organic cacao turns into decadent pudding. If you like dark, bittersweet flavors, this dessert may be right up your alley. If you're a milk-chocolate lover, serve it with cream, berries, and chopped almonds to cut the bitterness and balance every bite. This pudding is best consumed the day it's made, as the avocados will oxidize and the flavors will change over time.

dark chocolate pudding

SERVES 4 TO 6

1 cup (240ml) unsweetened almond milk (strained if homemade)

2 ripe avocados, pitted and peeled (see note, below)

1/3 cup (23g) plus 1 tablespoon cacao powder or unsweetened cocoa powder

1/2 cup (120ml) plus 2 table-spoons pure maple syrup or other natural liquid sweetener (see page 39)

2 teaspoons alcohol-free vanilla extract

1/4 teaspoon alcohol-free almond extract

1/4 teaspoon ground cinnamon

Pinch of natural salt (see box, page 38)

Cashew Cream (page 200), to garnish

1 cup (160g) fresh berries of your choice, to garnish

2 tablespoons blanched slivered raw almonds, roughly chopped, to garnish

Put the almond milk, avocados, cacao powder, maple syrup, vanilla and almond extracts, cinnamon, and salt into your blender and puree on high for 30 to 60 seconds, until smooth and creamy. (To get the creamiest texture, you may need to stop the machine and scrape down the sides of the container.) Transfer the pudding to cocktail glasses or ramekins, cover, and chill in the fridge for at least 3 hours.

To serve, top each pudding with a dollop of cream, a few fresh berries, and some almonds.

note: This pudding works best with ripe avocados that don't have any brown discolorations. Overripe or bruised avocados detract from the taste.

cacao

To get my chocolate fix, I use cacao powder. With an impressive antioxidant profile, cacao is rich in magnesium and a good source of calcium, iron, zinc, and potassium. Pure cacao beans, nibs, and powder contain no added sugar and are fabulous blended into nut milks, smoothies, and desserts. Note that you can substitute unsweetened cocoa powder in any of my recipes that call for cacao powder.

When I was making this simple and delicious sorbet one night, my partner Scott said, "You've got champagne and berries. How can you go wrong?" I couldn't agree more. The champagne keeps the mixture soft and slightly creamy when frozen and adds a subtle kick. For an alcohol-free version, use coconut water in place of the sparkling wine and reduce the sweetener by half. The consistency will be icier, but the sorbet will still be *berry* good.

sparkling black and blue

MAKES 1 QUART (1L)

1¼ cups (212g) fresh blackberries

1¼ cups (212g) fresh blueberries

½ cup (120ml) freshly squeezed orange juice

1 tablespoon freshly squeezed lemon juice

¼ cup (60ml) coconut nectar or other liquid natural sweetener (see page 39)

1 tablespoon coconut oil in liquid form

Pinch of natural salt (see box, page 38)

2 cups (480ml) dry sparkling white wine (dry or brut champagne or prosecco work well)

Throw the berries, juices, sweetener, coconut oil, and salt into your blender and puree on high for about 1 minute, until everything is smooth and incorporated. Transfer the mixture to a large glass bowl and chill in the fridge for about 3 hours, until thickened.

Remove the bowl from the fridge and stir in the sparkling wine. Use a whisk to break up any lumps. Churn the sorbet in an ice cream maker according to the manufacturer's instructions, and then freeze for at least 8 hours. The sorbet will get icier the longer it remains in the freezer. Scoop out and devour.

I love a bowl of delicious mint chip ice cream. This version is easy to throw together, and it has a rich creaminess that's reminiscent of full-fat dairy varieties. The last time my friend Stacey (a fellow ice cream devotee) and I made this, she told me (as we inhaled the whole batch in one sitting) that I was being "a bit stash" on the chocolate. Feel free to add more chocolate chips, lest you be accused of scrimping. If you don't have an ice cream maker, simply freeze the mixture, blend it again, freeze and blend it once more, and then freeze it a third time. Don't be put off by the spinach juice; you won't taste it, and it's a fabulously natural way to put the *green* in ice cream.

mint chip ice cream

MAKES 1 1/4 QUARTS (1.18L)

1 cup (43g) firmly packed baby spinach

1/3 cup (80ml) water

3 cups (720ml) canned coconut milk (shake, then pour)

3/4 cup (180ml) unsweetened almond or soy milk (strained if homemade)

1/2 cup (120ml) raw light agave or other light-colored sweetener (see note, below)

1 1/2 teaspoons peppermint extract, plus more to taste

1 teaspoon natural vanilla extract

1/4 cup (5g) mint leaves

3/4 cup (120g) finely chopped vegan chocolate or semi-sweet chocolate chips

Put the spinach and water into your blender and blend on high for about 20 seconds, until well combined. Strain the juice through a fine-mesh sieve. Measure out and reserve 3 tablespoons of the juice; reserve any remaining juice and the pulp fiber for a smoothie.

Pour the milks, agave nectar, extracts, and mint leaves into your blender and blast on high for about 1 minute, until combined. Add the spinach juice and blend again. Pour the mixture into a bowl and chill in the fridge for at least 4 hours, until really cold.

Churn in an ice cream maker according to the manufacturer's instructions, and in the last 10 minutes, add the chocolate. Freeze for at least 12 hours before serving.

note: If you use a dark-colored sweetener, the ice cream will turn an unpalatable brown color.

My mum has been making her incredible blender pecan pie for thirty years. I remember many a dinner party during my childhood, when guests arrived, poked their noses in the door, and said, "Please tell us you've made your pecan pie." Cut to Mum frantically grabbing the blender and Dad pouring cocktails to drown the disappointment, until the sweet smell of success wafted out of the oven. This flourless vegan spin on my mum's classic just might be better than the old favorite. It's a pie and a cake at once, and while it's a bit more fiddly than my mother's blend-bake-and-chow dessert, it's dairy- and egg-free, and oh so good. Share this pecan pleasure at your next party and you'll have guests clamoring for more.

flourless triple-pecan mousse pie

SERVES 8 TO 10

crust

1 cup (110g) raw pecans

1½ teaspoons coconut oil in liquid form

¼ teaspoon natural vanilla extract

2 tablespoons coconut sugar or other granulated natural sugar (see page 39)

1½ teaspoons water

filling

¾ cup (180ml) water

1¼ cups (300ml) canned coconut milk (shake, then pour)

2 cups (280g) raw unsalted cashews, soaked (see page 22)

½ cup (120ml) pure maple syrup

¼ cup (38g) coconut sugar

2¼ cups (248g) raw pecans

2 teaspoons natural vanilla extract

2 tablespoons arrowroot

2 tablespoons ground flaxseeds

¼ teaspoon natural salt (see box, page 38)

candied pecans

2 cups (220g) raw pecans

⅓ cup (80ml) pure maple syrup

2 teaspoons water

Pinch of natural salt

maple-pecan cream

1 cup (240g) reserved cashew cream (from filling)

½ teaspoon natural vanilla extract

¼ cup (28g) raw pecans

2 tablespoons pure maple syrup

Pinch of natural salt

To make the crust, line the bottom of a 9-inch (23cm) springform pan with a parchment paper round that has been cut to fit. Put all of the ingredients into your food processor and pulse until the mixture has the consistency of breadcrumbs and is pulling away from the sides of the container. Press the crust into the bottom of the prepared pan and place the pan in the fridge to chill for 30 minutes.

Preheat the oven to 325°F (160°C).

To make the filling, pour the water, ¼ cup of the coconut milk, and the cashews into your blender and blast on high for 1 to 2 minutes (or a bit longer if you're using a conventional blender), until smooth and creamy. (Add a tiny bit more water as necessary to blend, but keep in mind that you want the cashew cream to be super thick.) Transfer the cream to a bowl and wash your blender.

Spoon 1¹/₄ cups (300g) of the cashew cream back into your blender and reserve the rest in the fridge for making the maple-pecan cream. Add the maple syrup, coconut sugar, pecans, vanilla, arrowroot, flaxseeds, salt, and the remaining 1 cup of coconut milk into your blender and puree for 30 to 60 seconds, until thick and creamy.

Remove the chilled crust from the fridge and pour the filling into the crust. Gently wiggle the pan to ensure a uniform top. Set the springform pan on a baking sheet and bake the pie for 1 hour, until just slightly browned on the edges and still a bit wobbly in the center. Transfer the pie to a cooling rack and cool completely. Cover the pie and chill it thoroughly in the fridge, at least 8 hours or overnight.

To make the candied pecans (see photo, page 150), preheat the oven to 350°F (180°C). Toast the pecans on a baking sheet lined with parchment paper for 10 minutes, until crispy and fragrant. In a small saucepan over medium-low heat, combine the maple syrup, water, and salt and cook for 5 minutes, stirring constantly, until the mixture starts to bubble and caramelize. Stir in the warm pecans and cook for 3 to 4 minutes, until the nuts caramelize and the liquid has completely evaporated. The nuts should be almost dry and the maple sugar should crystallize. Return the nuts to the parchment paper–lined baking sheet and let them cool to room temperature.

To make the maple-pecan cream, pour 1 cup (240g) of the reserved cashew cream into your blender and add the vanilla, pecans, maple syrup, and salt. Blend on high for 1 to 2 minutes, until creamy.

Remove the pie from the fridge and pour the maple-pecan cream over the top. Place the candied pecans on top of the cashew cream in a decorative design (whole or crushed candied pecans, in a fan design, or whatever your preference). Return the pie to the fridge for 2 hours more, to firm it up again. Remove the sides of the springform pan. Using a serrated knife, cut the pie into slices and serve chilled.

This pie is alkaline, sugar-free, and guilt-free, so no one has to miss out on the fun. This was my partner, Scott's, favorite indulgence when he was being treated for cancer and couldn't eat anything sweeter than a carrot. See the variation below if you don't like the taste of stevia. When I'm feeling lazy, we enjoy this filling as a crustless dessert or a butter.

sugar-free no-pumpkin pie

SERVES 8 TO 10

crust

1¹/₂ cups (240g) raw whole almonds

³/₄ cup (75g) shredded unsweetened coconut

3 tablespoons coconut oil in liquid form

1 tablespoon water

¹/₂ teaspoon alcohol-free vanilla extract

15 drops each Sweet Leaf Vanilla Crème alcohol-free liquid stevia and Sweet Leaf English Toffee alcohol-free liquid stevia (see page 39)

filling

1 cup (240ml) strained carrot juice

³/₄ cup (180ml) coconut oil in liquid form

1 cup (140g) blanched slivered raw almonds, soaked (see page 22)

1 cup (180g) young Thai coconut meat (see note, page 200)

¹/₄ cup (60g) raw almond butter

40 drops Sweet Leaf English Toffee alcohol-free liquid stevia

1 teaspoon alcohol-free vanilla extract

2 teaspoons ground cinnamon

³/₄ teaspoon ground nutmeg

¹/₂ teaspoon ground ginger

Pinch of ground cloves

Pinch of natural salt (see box, page 38)

Raw pumpkin seeds, to garnish

To make the crust, line a 9-inch (23cm) pie plate with enough plastic wrap to snugly cover the bottom and generously hang over the edges of the plate to help release the pie after chilling. Put the almonds, shredded coconut, coconut oil, water, vanilla, and stevia into a food processor and pulse until the mixture has the consistency of breadcrumbs and pulls away from the sides of the container. Press the mixture evenly into the bottom and sides of the pie plate. Chill for 1 to 2 hours, until firm.

To make the filling, throw all of the ingredients into your blender and blast on high for about 2 minutes, until smooth and creamy. (If using a high-speed blender, be careful of overblending or the mixture will get too warm.) Pour the filling into the chilled crust and jiggle the pie plate slightly to even out the top. Chill for at least 8 hours, and preferably overnight.

To serve, sprinkle the pie with pumpkin seeds. Lift the plastic wrap gently to release the pie from the plate, then slide the pie back into the plate. Using a very sharp knife, cut slices and serve.

variation: Replace the stevia in the crust with 2 tablespoons of coconut sugar. For the filling, replace the stevia with ¹/₄ cup (38g) of coconut sugar and increase the spices to 1 tablespoon of cinnamon, 1 teaspoon of nutmeg, 1 teaspoon of ginger, and a generous pinch of cloves.

CHAPTER 9

drinks, juices & tonics

My friends Sue and George sampled a mind-altering sangria in Spain, and learned that the secret ingredient was a vanilla bean. I stole that idea, and blended pineapple juice with fresh pineapple to avoid adding sweetener. What brings these flavors and the wine together is Grand Marnier. Triple Sec just doesn't cut it. This blend needs to sit for at least 24 hours for the flavors to mature. I'm gonna be bold and say that this is the best sangria I've ever tasted. But maybe I don't get out much.

pineapple vanilla sangria

SERVES 6

1 1/2 cups (360ml) unsweetened pineapple juice

2 cups (320g) diced pineapple (or canned, in natural juice with no added sugar)

1 (750ml) bottle Cabernet Sauvignon or Cabernet-Merlot blend

1/4 cup (60ml) brandy

1/4 cup (60ml) Grand Marnier

1 orange

1 ripe pear, cored and diced

1/2 vanilla bean, sliced lengthwise (seeds intact)

10 mint leaves (optional)

2 cups (250g) ice, to serve (optional)

Throw the pineapple juice and 1 cup (160g) of the diced pineapple into your blender and puree on high for 30 to 60 seconds, until creamy. In a glass pitcher or punch bowl, combine the wine, brandy, and Grand Marnier. Stir the pineapple blend into the wine mixture (don't be concerned about the frothiness; it settles).

Cut the orange in half vertically, and then cut each half into 8 to 10 slices, discarding the ends. Add the orange slices, along with the remaining 1 cup (160g) of diced pineapple, the pears, vanilla bean, and mint to the sangria. Stir to combine and let sit at room temperature for 8 to 12 hours, until the fruit flavors have infused the mix. Chill in the fridge for 12 to 24 hours.

To serve, remove the vanilla bean and half of the orange slices (too much fruit can be overwhelming). If serving all the sangria at once, add all of the ice to the pitcher. Otherwise, drop ice into individual glasses.

My favorite margarita enthusiast, George, took one sip of this cocktail and said decisively, "Needs Grand Marnier!" I replied, "Who doesn't?" You *can* use another orange-flavored liquor like Cointreau or Triple Sec, but Grand Marnier, along with the quality of your tequila, is what puts this in a different league.

virgin-or-not peach margarita

SERVES 2

¼ cup (60ml) unsweetened pineapple juice

¼ cup (60ml) freshly squeezed lime juice

2 cups (320g) chopped frozen peaches

¼ cup (60ml) tequila, plus more to taste

2 tablespoons Grand Marnier

1 tablespoon agave nectar, plus more to taste

1 cup (125g) ice, plus more as needed

Lime wedges, to garnish (optional)

1 tablespoon medium-coarse natural salt (optional)

Finely grated lime zest, to garnish (optional)

Throw the pineapple juice, lime juice, peaches, tequila, Grand Marnier, agave nectar, and ice cubes into your blender and blast on high for 30 to 60 seconds, until well combined. You may need to stop the machine to help guide the ingredients through the blades. Tweak flavors to taste (you may like more agave nectar or alcohol) and add more ice cubes if you want a slushier consistency.

To serve, run the lime wedge around the rims of two margarita glasses. Pour the salt and zest into a shallow saucer and carefully dip the glass rims into the mixture. Divide the blend between the glasses.

My friend Kim summed up this piña colada: "Seems like a really healthy way to drink alcohol!" That said, this rich, creamy blend can be enjoyed with or without rum (see the variation below for a version sans alcohol). Adjust the amount of sweetener according to the ripeness of your pineapple. If your pineapple is very ripe, or you're making this without rum, you may want to hold off on the sweetener until you give the blend a taste. But, I find that a small amount of sweetener rounds out the flavors.

simple or strong piña colada

SERVES 2

3/4 cup (180ml) canned coconut milk (shake, then pour)

1/2 cup (120ml) unsweetened pineapple juice

1 cup (160g) diced ripe pineapple

1 cup (160g) frozen diced pineapple

1/2 teaspoon natural vanilla extract

3 tablespoons white rum, plus more to taste (optional)

1 teaspoon pure maple syrup, plus more to taste (optional)

1 cup (125g) ice cubes

Pineapple wedges, to garnish

Throw all of the ingredients into your blender and puree for 30 to 60 seconds, until smooth. Tweak the rum and maple syrup to taste. Serve with a wedge of pineapple.

variation: Use alcohol-free vanilla extract and replace the rum with 1/2 cup (7g) of loosely packed dandelion greens. These nutrient-dense greens have a slight bitterness that gives the drink a hint of alcohol flavor.

This sugar-free drink is incredibly refreshing on a hot day. A good and ripe melon dramatically improves the flavor. Chill this well before serving; warm agua fresca never rocks anyone's world. Add a touch of gin or vodka for a fabulous summer cocktail.

spike-it-if-you-like minty melon agua fresca

SERVES 4

1 cup (240ml) coconut water

4 cups (600g) chopped ripe honeydew melon

2 tablespoons freshly squeezed lemon juice

20 mint leaves

Natural liquid sweetener (optional; see page 39)

Ice, to serve

Throw the coconut water, melon, lemon juice, and mint leaves into your blender and blast on high for about 1 minute, until well combined and smooth. Have a sip and add sweetener to taste. Strain the mixture through a fine-mesh sieve or nut milk bag. Discard the pulp and chill the agua fresca for at least 2 hours and up to 2 days. Serve over ice.

variation: Add 1/2 cup (120ml) gin or vodka and blend along with the rest of the ingredients. Taste and add more alcohol if you like.

I decided to perfect this blend on a lazy Sunday morning with my Bloody Mary–lovin' friends, Mika and Denise. We like our ladies rustic. If you prefer a smooth drink, add some water or tomato juice and strain. There's a brand of vegan Worcestershire sauce made by Annie's (see Resources, page 209) that is fabulous in this drink. For a gluten-free *and* vegan option, The Wizard's brand from Edward & Sons is available online. This is a great hangover cure, or, without the vodka, a great morning pick-me-up. Either way, Mary rocks.

rustic, bold or bloody mary

SERVES 2

2 cups (300g) chopped tomato (about 2 tomatoes)

1 tablespoon tomato paste

1/2 cup (66g) diced celery (about 2 ribs)

2 teaspoons minced fresh horseradish (not horseradish sauce), plus more to taste

2 teaspoons Worcestershire sauce, plus more to taste

3 dashes of Tabasco sauce, plus more to taste

1 tablespoon freshly squeezed lemon juice, plus more to taste

1 teaspoon finely chopped red onion

1 clove garlic

Natural salt (see box, page 38)

Freshly ground black pepper

1 lemon wedge, to garnish (optional)

Ice cubes, to serve

1/4 cup (60ml) vodka

2 inner celery ribs with leaves, to garnish

Throw the chopped tomato, tomato paste, celery, horseradish, Worcestershire, Tabasco, lemon juice, onion, garlic, 3/4 teaspoon of salt, and 3/8 teaspoon of pepper into your blender and blast on high for about 1 minute, until fully pureed. Tweak flavors to taste (you may want more horseradish, Worcestershire, Tabasco, lemon juice, salt, or pepper). I drink this unstrained, but you can pass it through a fine-mesh sieve if you want, pushing the mix in with a spoon and discarding the pulp. Keep the Bloody Mary mix in the fridge until ready to serve.

To serve, run the lemon wedge around the rims of two highball glasses. Pour a mixture of salt and pepper into a shallow saucer and dip the glass rims into the mix. Divide the ice and vodka between the glasses and add the Bloody Mary mix. Garnish each glass with a celery stalk and serve.

Forget saving this for the holidays! I could drink it every day of the week and twice on Sunday. It's *so* delicious, and unbelievably rich and creamy (as long as you soak the nuts). You won't believe this doesn't contain dairy. You can enjoy this as a dessert drink or a festive toaster with or without the alcohol (see the variation below), but the brandy is just dandy.

holiday eggnog

SERVES 4 TO 6

2 cups (480ml) unsweetened almond milk (strained if homemade)

1/4 cup (60ml) canned coconut milk (shake, then pour)

1/2 cup (70g) raw unsalted cashews, soaked (see page 22)

3 ounces (85g) soft silken tofu

1 ripe banana

1/2 teaspoon natural vanilla extract

1/4 cup (60ml) pure maple syrup

3/4 teaspoon ground cinnamon, plus more to garnish

1/2 teaspoon freshly grated nutmeg, plus more to garnish

Pinch of ground cloves

Pinch of natural salt (see box, page 38)

1/4 cup (60ml) brandy

Throw all of the ingredients (except the brandy) into your blender and puree on high for 1 to 2 minutes, until smooth and creamy. Add the brandy and blast again briefly to combine. Chill the eggnog in a glass container in the fridge for at least 3 hours so the flavors can settle and so the mixture thickens slightly. (If you're in a hurry, you can blend in some ice.)

Serve chilled, dusted with cinnamon, nutmeg, or a bit of both. The eggnog will keep in the fridge for 2 days, but it is best consumed the day it's made.

variation: To make a non-alcoholic version, add 2 additional tablespoons of raw unsalted cashews, soaked; decrease the amount of pure maple syrup to 2 to 3 tablespoons to taste; use alcohol-free vanilla extract; and omit the brandy.

Chocolate and hazelnuts are meant to live together in a glass. Hot or cold, this milk is a delicious, decadent drink. I've deliberately made this quite sweet, but you can adjust the amount of dates to your taste. Likewise, add the cacao powder to your preference. I like to taste as much of the hazelnuts as possible, so I keep the chocolate in check. But if you feel the opposite, just double the chocolate. This drink can be tweaked to taste before you strain to get it *juuuuust* right.

hot chocolate with hazelnuts

SERVES 2

1 cup (150g) raw hazelnuts, soaked (see page 22)

3 cups (720ml) water

½ cup (90g) firmly packed chopped pitted dates, soaked (see page 22), plus more to taste

3 tablespoons cacao powder or unsweetened cocoa powder, plus more to taste

1 teaspoon alcohol-free vanilla extract

Gluten-free vegan mini marshmallows, or regular mini marshmallows, to serve (optional)

Throw the hazelnuts, water, dates, cacao powder, and vanilla into your blender and blast on high for 1 to 2 minutes, until the nuts and dates are pulverized and the mixture is smooth. Tweak flavors to taste (you may want more dates or chocolate). Strain the mixture through a nut milk bag or fine-mesh sieve into a small saucepan.

Set the saucepan over low to medium heat and gently warm for 3 to 4 minutes, until the mixture is hot. (Don't let it boil or it may separate.) Serve in mugs topped with the marshmallows.

variation: To serve cold, chill in the fridge or pour over ice cubes.

fruity lemonade 3 ways

When the universe gives you lemons, make low-sugar, fruit-sweetened lemonade! Here are some of my favorite combinations. I love rustic, unstrained lemonade, but it's not for everyone. Strain these if you want a pulp-free drink. And be sure to chill the drinks in the fridge before pouring them over ice; otherwise, the lemonade gets diluted. Get creative; the sky's the limit.

strawberry-basil

SERVES 2 TO 4

2 cups (480ml) water

1/2 cup (120ml) freshly squeezed lemon juice, plus more to taste

3 cups (480g) chopped strawberries

1/3 cup (80ml) agave nectar, plus more to taste

1/4 cup (22g) firmly packed basil

Throw all of the ingredients into your blender and blast on high for 1 minute, until well combined. Tweak flavors to taste (you may want more lemon juice or agave nectar). Strain through a fine-mesh sieve or nut milk bag, chill, and serve.

pineapple-ginger

SERVES 2

2 cups (480ml) water

1/2 cup (120ml) freshly squeezed lemon juice, plus more to taste

3 cups (480g) diced ripe pineapple, plus more to taste

1 tablespoon minced ginger

2 tablespoons agave nectar, plus more to taste

Throw all of the ingredients into your blender and blast on high for about 1 minute, until well combined. Tweak flavors to taste (you may want more lemon juice, pineapple, or agave nectar). Strain through a fine-mesh sieve or nut milk bag, chill, and serve.

grape-mint

SERVES 2 TO 4

2 cups (480ml) water

1/2 cup (120ml) freshly squeezed lemon juice, plus more to taste

4 cups (680g) green seedless grapes

15 mint leaves

1 tablespoon agave nectar, or 10 drops alcohol-free liquid stevia, plus more to taste

Throw all of the ingredients into your blender and blast on high for 1 minute, until well combined. Tweak flavors to taste (you may want more lemon juice or sweetener). Strain through a fine-mesh sieve or nut milk bag, chill, and serve.

rose water

When roses and water are distilled to make rose oil, rose water is left over. You can find 100 percent rose water at health food stores and Middle Eastern grocers for a few dollars. Steer clear of the blends with added water and flavoring, and of rose syrups, which are loaded with refined sugar, citric acid, and flavorings.

I love a good lassi. My body, however, does not like the dairy. This vegan version is a great compromise, and it more than holds its own against traditional recipes. Although you can use any kind of yogurt you like, I find that dairy-free yogurt never really has the tang of its dairy counterpart. This is where the lemon juice comes in. Add more juice to get the right level of tang. (If you use a traditional kefir, you won't need the lemon juice at all.) The combination of rose water and cardamom is something special.

rose water–cardamom lassi

SERVES 2

1 cup (240g) coconut milk yogurt, or any vegan yogurt or kefir

1/2 cup (120ml) canned coconut milk (shake, then pour), or any milk or kefir

2 fresh or frozen sliced bananas

2 cups (250g) ice cubes, plus more to serve

1/2 teaspoon ground cardamom (see note, page 161)

1 teaspoon pure distilled rose water (see note, opposite page)

1 teaspoon freshly squeezed lemon juice, plus more to taste

1 pitted and soaked (see page 22) date, plus more to taste, or other natural sweetener (see page 39)

Throw all of the ingredients into your blender and puree for 30 to 60 seconds, until smooth and creamy. Tweak flavors to taste (you may like more lemon juice or sweetener). Serve as is or over ice.

Most juice-based cold and flu remedies are mixtures of lemon juice, honey, and cayenne. This carrot juice blend is an interesting alternative to the ubiquitous (albeit highly effective) lemon juice tonics. Loaded with some of the top immunity-boosting foods, this tonic packs a fiery punch, and is yummy to boot.

beat-the-cold-and-flu blues

SERVES 1

1 1/2 cups (360ml) water

2 carrots, peeled and roughly chopped

1/2 large or 1 small green apple, cored and chopped

1 tablespoon freshly squeezed lemon juice

2 teaspoons minced ginger

1/8 teaspoon ground cinnamon

Pinch of cayenne pepper

5 drops alcohol-free liquid stevia (see page 39)

Throw all of the ingredients into your blender and blast on high for 30 to 60 seconds, until everything is completely pulverized. Drink this straight, chilled, or over ice. You can also strain it through a fine-mesh sieve first (the cayenne will be a lot milder when strained).

You can make juice in your blender in minutes. I drink this alkalizing juice almost every week for an amazing pick-me-up. You may need to add more water, depending on the size of your fruit. And if you like sweet juice, add an extra apple. The cayenne is extremely cleansing, but add it with a light hand or this baby might blow your head off!

green alkalaid

SERVES 1

1 cup (240ml) water or coconut water, plus more as needed

2 cups (54g) loosely packed baby spinach

2 small lemons, peeled, quartered, and seeded

1 cucumber, peeled and roughly chopped

1 or 2 green apples, cored and chopped

1 teaspoon finely chopped ginger

2 drops alcohol-free liquid stevia (see page 39), plue more to taste

Pinch of cayenne pepper, plus more to taste (optional)

Throw all of the ingredients into your blender and puree on high for 1 to 2 minutes, until smooth. Add more water as needed until you have the consistency of a thin smoothie; if you're using 2 apples, you'll definitely need more water. Tweak flavors to taste (you may want more stevia and cayenne). Strain through a fine-mesh sieve and drink chilled or over ice.

This blend is cleansing and delicious, and it contains some of the top skin-boosting foods. I brew the tea for the base quite strong so it stands up to the other flavors. Drink this blend on a regular basis and your skin will love you.

skin sing

SERVES 1

2 green tea bags

1¹/₂ cups (360ml) boiling water

2 kiwis, peeled and roughly chopped

¹/₂ large or 1 small green apple, cored and chopped

1 cup (43g) firmly packed baby spinach

1 teaspoon flaxseed oil

1 tablespoon freshly squeezed lemon juice, plus more to taste

Pinch of finely grated lemon zest, plus more to taste

5 drops alcohol-free liquid stevia (see page 39), plus more to taste

In a small bowl, steep the tea bags in the boiling water for about 3 minutes. Remove the bags and allow the tea to cool.

Put the cooled tea and the remaining ingredients into your blender and puree on high for 1 to 2 minutes, until well combined. Tweak flavors to taste (you might like more lemon juice, zest, and sweetener). Strain through a fine-mesh sieve or nut milk bag and chill.

variation: For a raw drink, steep the green tea in cold water.

This drink is a fantastic way to get your daily dose of probiotics. I make it often because it's tasty, low in sugar, alkaline-forming, and loaded with beneficial bacteria. If you've been looking for a probiotic drink, but don't like the flavor of kefir, this may be the answer. (Try making your own kefir so you can control the flavor; see page 28.) The addition of almond milk to this tonic makes it taste like a milkshake. To sweeten this up for kids, add a banana or some maple syrup, coconut nectar, or dates. But to get the full effects of the probiotics, it's best to use stevia. Boosting this shake with a mild leafy green like spinach (a fabulous prebiotic) helps to support the probiotic power.

probiotic kefir sweeper

SERVES 1

1 cup (240ml) unsweetened almond milk (strained if homemade)

1 cup (240ml) almond or coconut milk kefir (see page 28)

1 1/2 cups (240g) fresh or frozen strawberries

1 tablespoon raw almond butter

1 teaspoon shelled hemp seeds

1 teaspoon black or white chia seeds

1 teaspoon ground flaxseeds

1 teaspoon alcohol-free vanilla extract

1/4 teaspoon probiotic powder (see note, page 30)

1/4 teaspoon finely grated lemon zest

1/8 teaspoon ground cinnamon

Pinch of natural salt (see box, page 38)

20 drops alcohol-free liquid stevia or other natural sweetener (see page 39)

1 cup (125g) ice cubes (optional; omit if using frozen berries)

Throw all of the ingredients into your blender and blast on high for about 1 minute, until smooth and creamy.

Dubbed "nature's Gatorade," coconut water is a natural isotonic drink that contains more electrolytes than most commercial sports drinks. When you combine it with the extraordinary power of chia seeds, you have a massive energy booster. This sugar-free, fat-free workout beverage, which was inspired by one of my readers, Marie-Guy, will help you maintain your body's electrolyte balance. It's low in calories, but rich in vitamins B and C, potassium, magnesium, calcium, iron, and zinc. The chia will also help you replenish minerals you've lost during exercise.

You can flavor this basic mixture with a variety of fruits. However, I prefer this alkalizing blend. I find the flavor of ginger too intense for exercising. However, many friends enjoy it in this drink. To get the best consistency, make this a couple of hours before you drink it and let it chill. The chia seeds will swell a bit but won't thicken the blend to the point of sludge. I drink this when I work out, but also as an all-around health elixir to boost my liver, thyroid, kidney, and gall bladder function. Did I mention its beautifying powers? This is also great for your skin.

chia choo choo!

SERVES 1

2 cups (480ml) coconut water

1 teaspoon finely grated lime zest

¼ cup (60ml) freshly squeezed orange juice

2 tablespoons freshly squeezed lemon juice

2 tablespoons freshly squeezed lime juice

2 tablespoons black or white chia seeds

Alcohol-free liquid stevia or other natural sweetener (optional; see page 39)

Throw the coconut water, lime zest, and juices into your blender and blast on high for 30 to 60 seconds, until the zest has been pulverized and evenly distributed. Add the chia seeds and blend on low (if you're using a high-speed blender) or high (if you're using a conventional blender) for just a few seconds, until the chia is incorporated and slightly broken down but not fully blended. Taste, add about 5 drops of stevia or to taste, and blend again briefly. Transfer the mixture to a glass jar and chill it in the fridge for at least 2 hours. (If you used chilled liquids to begin with, you can drink this right away for an immediate boost, but the chia will be gritty.) Give it a stir before drinking.

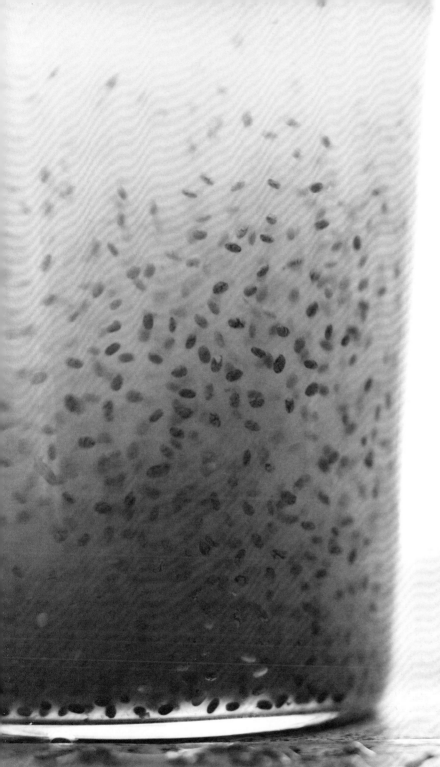

chia seeds

Chia is a miraculous superfood. It's the richest plant-based source of omega-3 fatty acids, is high in calcium and magnesium, and has a complete amino acid profile, loads of fiber, and a truckload of antioxidants. Whether you use black or white chia seeds, their mild and nutty flavor won't alter the flavor of your blends when used in small amounts. Sprinkle them over cereals, salads, stir-fries, curries, and soups. Chia's binding and gelling quality is part of its magic. Chia assists the body with retaining fluids and electrolytes, helps to lower the glycemic index of foods, aids in the absorption of calcium, and contributes to muscle and tissue building and colon health. The seeds absorb up to nine times their weight in liquid and gain a smooth viscosity. This quality makes chia an ideal binder for burgers and patties or for pancakes (see page 146) and other baked goods. You can also use chia to make nutritious puddings (see page 163) or thicken jams (see page 83).

To make a chia gel: Whisk 2 tablespoons of chia seeds into 1 cup (240ml) of water and store in a sealed glass jar in the fridge for up to 1 week. This gel can be added to smoothies, soups, sauces, and desserts.

If you suffer from acid reflux, this simple flaxseed tea may be your new best friend. This drink is also an excellent way to support your general colon health. I use golden flaxseeds here because they have a milder flavor than brown. Plain flaxseed tea can be a bit unpalatable, but the addition of ginger, lemon juice, and stevia makes this one delicious.

acid reflux be gone

SERVES 1

1½ cups (360ml) boiling water

1 tablespoon golden flaxseeds

1-inch (2.5cm) piece ginger root, cut into 4 slices, plus more to taste

2 tablespoons freshly squeezed lemon juice, plus more to taste

5 drops alcohol-free liquid stevia (see page 39), plus more to taste

Pour the boiling water over the flaxseeds, ginger, and lemon juice and allow the tea to steep for 30 to 60 minutes (the longer you steep, the more pronounced the ginger flavor will be; if you really love ginger, add up to 2 more slices before steeping). Pour the flaxseeds, ginger slices, and the tea into your blender and blast on high for about 1 minute. Stir in the stevia to taste and then strain the mixture through a fine-mesh sieve. Tweak flavors to taste again (you may want more lemon juice or stevia). Drink at room temperature, or warm gently over low heat.

Turmeric milk has been a favorite in India for years, and for good reason. The spice is a powerful anti-inflammatory, and it can relieve cold and flu symptoms and settle the stomach. This magical, healing drink is also a fabulous way to relax and calm the body, and assist with sleep. Oh, and did I mention that this blend is just plain yummy? It's my ultimate bedtime comfort food.

sleep spell

SERVES 1

1 cup (240g) unsweetened almond milk (strained if homemade)

1 tablespoon raw unsalted cashews, blanched slivered raw almonds, or shelled raw pistachios, soaked (see page 22)

1 teaspoon ground cinnamon

1/4 teaspoon ground turmeric

1/4 teaspoon minced ginger

Pinch of ground cardamom (optional; see note, page 161)

2 pitted soaked (see page 22) dates, or 5 drops alcohol-free liquid stevia (see page 39)

Throw all of the ingredients into your blender and blast on high for 1 to 2 minutes, until the dates are fully incorporated. Strain the mixture through a fine-mesh sieve into a saucepan. Set the saucepan over low heat for 1 to 2 minutes, until the mixture is just warm. (Alternatively, if you're using a high-speed blender, just keep blending until the mixture is warm, and then strain it right into your glass.)

CHAPTER 10

condiments, sauces & creams

This simple, healthy version tastes pretty close to the commercial varieties that some people like to slap on everything. If you're one of them, fear not, as this ketchup skips the sugar and preservatives. I've deliberately kept this recipe simple to approximate the familiar brands, but you can jazz it up with your pick of spices for a more exotic blend. After a night in the fridge, the flavor is superb, and with a bit of chilling, the ketchup will thicken. If you like your ketchup thicker, use the optional cornstarch, arrowroot, or kuzu-root powder. With regards to Worcestershire sauce, The Wizard's is a great gluten-free vegan brand; if you're not gluten free, Annie's Naturals has a fabulous vegan option (see Resources, page 209). Whip up a batch of this ketchup and you may want to have it with everything, too.

i'll have ketchup with that

MAKES 1¹/₂ CUPS (400G)

2 (14.5-ounce/411g) cans unsalted diced or crushed tomatoes

2 tablespoons tomato paste

¹/₃ cup (50g) diced red onion

2 cloves garlic, roughly chopped

2¹/₂ tablespoons pure maple syrup

2¹/₂ tablespoons apple cider vinegar

¹/₂ teaspoon gluten-free, vegan, or regular Worcestershire sauce

¹/₂ teaspoon natural salt (see box, page 38)

Pinch of yellow mustard powder

Pinch of freshly ground black pepper

1 teaspoon cornstarch or arrowroot, or ¹/₂ teaspoon kuzu-root powder (see Resources, page 209) plus 1 teaspoon water, as needed to thicken (optional)

Throw the canned tomatoes and their juices, the tomato paste, onion, garlic, maple syrup, vinegar, Worcestershire sauce, salt, mustard powder, and pepper into your blender and puree on high for about 1 minute, until well combined and smooth. Transfer the mixture to a saucepan over high heat and bring it just to a boil. Reduce the heat to medium and simmer, stirring occasionally, for about 30 minutes, until the mixture has reduced and thickened to your preference. (It will thicken more with chilling, but if you think you'd like it even thicker, combine the cornstarch and water in a small bowl to make a paste. Stir the paste into the tomato mixture and simmer for 10 to 15 minutes more, until thickened.)

Remove the pan from the heat and let the ketchup cool to room temperature. Transfer it to a glass container, seal tightly, and place it in the fridge. The ketchup will keep in the fridge for up to 1 month.

I love this sauce because you can blend it up quickly, and you don't need to cook it. With sweet and tangy flavors, plus a touch of smoke and heat, it always receives rave reviews, even from people who pooh-pooh barbecue. Slather it on grilled vegetables or burgers and you'll lick your fingers and make some more.

5-minute bbq sauce

MAKES 1 1/3 CUPS (360G)

1/2 cup (120ml) unsweetened, unfiltered apple juice

1/4 cup (60ml) pure maple syrup

2 tablespoons blackstrap molasses

1 (6-ounce/170g) can tomato paste

2 tablespoons wheat-free tamari or soy sauce

1 tablespoon stone-ground mustard

2 tablespoons apple cider vinegar

1 tablespoon freshly squeezed lemon juice

1 teaspoon minced garlic (about 1 clove)

1 1/4 teaspoons minced ginger

1/2 teaspoon onion powder

1/8 teaspoon freshly ground black pepper

1/8 teaspoon chili powder

1/8 teaspoon natural salt (see box, page 38)

Throw all of the ingredients into your blender and puree on high for about 1 minute, until smooth and well combined. The sauce can be stored in an airtight container in the fridge for up to 5 days.

This raw, non-egg mayo with a mild, well-rounded flavor makes a great base for all kinds of dressings and sauces, and for staple dishes like my Creamy and Crunchy Spuds (page 88). Every batch yields a mayo with a slightly different personality. Depending on my mood and my plans for using the mayo, I often pour in the lemon juice, vinegar, and salt separately at the end, tasting between additions to get it just right. Use any natural sweetener that suits, but make sure to soak the cashews to get the creamiest results. The addition of fresh herbs and greens can be delicious, and some garlic makes an awesome aioli. The possibilities are endless, but sometimes plain and simple works best.

i-use-it-in-everything raw mayo

MAKES 1¹/₃ CUPS (310G)

¹/₄ cup (60ml) water

1 cup (140g) raw unsalted cashews, soaked (see page 22)

¹/₄ cup (30g) chopped cauliflower florets

¹/₄ cup (60ml) cold-pressed extra-virgin olive oil

1¹/₄ teaspoons yellow mustard, plus more to taste

1 teaspoon apple cider vinegar, plus more to taste

3 tablespoons freshly squeezed lemon juice, plus more to taste

1 teaspoon coconut sugar, plus more to taste

¹/₄ teaspoon natural salt (see box, page 38), plus more to taste

Throw all of the ingredients into your blender and blast on high for 1 to 2 minutes, until smooth and creamy. You may have to stop the machine periodically and scrape down the sides of the container. Tweak flavors to taste (you may want more mustard, vinegar, lemon juice, sweetener, or salt). Store in a glass jar in the fridge for up to 5 days.

Fresh lime juice is the key to the fabulous balance in this blend. Many of my friends have reported eating it straight out of the jar! Like my other creams, this gets better after chilling.

slick sour cream

MAKES 1 CUP (250G)

1/4 cup (60ml) almond milk (strained if homemade), plus more as needed

1 tablespoon cold-pressed extra-virgin olive oil

2 1/2 tablespoons freshly squeezed lime juice, plus more to taste

1 1/2 tablespoons apple cider vinegar, plus more to taste

4 ounces (113g) firm silken tofu

1/2 cup (60g) blanched raw almonds, soaked (see page 22)

1 tablespoon white miso paste (see page 128)

3/4 teaspoon salt (see box, page 38), plus more to taste

1/4 teaspoon minced garlic

1 tablespoon finely chopped chives (optional)

Put the almond milk, olive oil, lime juice, and vinegar into your blender, then add the tofu, almonds, miso, salt, and garlic and blast on high for 1 to 2 minutes, until smooth and creamy. Add another tablespoon of almond milk as needed for smooth blending. Tweak flavors to taste (you may like more lime juice or vinegar). Transfer the blend to a small bowl, cover, and chill for a few hours, until the mixture thickens and the flavors meld.

Before using, stir in the chives. This will keep in the fridge for 2 to 3 days.

variations: To use raw unsalted cashews instead of almonds, reduce the amount of salt, lime juice, and vinegar just a tad to start, and then add to taste. With blanched almonds, natural salt really pulls the flavors together and helps to balance the tang. However, all salts are different, so if you're using cashews, start with 1/2 teaspoon and work up in pinches until you have the balance you like.

3 sweet cream dreams

Here are three of my favorite vegan creams. The cashew cream is a staple in our house, and you can also make it with almonds. For the tofu variety, I've disguised any soy aftertaste with a hit of citrus. The basic soy cream is a nice complement to most desserts, but the lemon variation is simply divine. The soy taste will intensify the longer it sits, so use it the day you make it. The alkaline sugar-free version ages like a fine wine. Given time, the stevia settles and the flavors mesh beautifully. For the cashew cream and the alkaline cream, you've gotta soak those nuts to get the smoothest consistency. We *are* talking about cream.

cashew cream

MAKES 1¼ CUPS (300G)

¾ cup (180ml) unsweetened almond milk (strained if homemade)

1 cup (140g) raw unsalted cashews, soaked (see page 22)

2 tablespoons pure maple syrup or coconut sugar

1½ teaspoons alcohol-free vanilla extract, plus more to taste

Pinch of finely grated lemon zest

Throw all of the ingredients into your blender and blast on high for 1 to 2 minutes, until smooth and creamy. You may need to stop the machine and scrape down the sides of the container to get the creamiest result. Tweak the vanilla to taste. Transfer to a bowl and chill in the fridge for a few hours to let the cream thicken slightly. It will keep in an airtight container in the fridge for up to 5 days.

variation: To make almond cream, increase the almond milk to 1 cup (240ml) and replace the cashews with 1 cup (120g) blanched slivered raw almonds, soaked (see page 22).

coconut meat

Incredibly alkalizing and full of healthy fats, oils, and immune-boosting goodness, young Thai coconut meat (which is soft and pliable) is fantastic for making homemade coconut milk, creaming up smoothies, and as a base for raw puddings, desserts, creams, and yogurt. I also use unsweetened dried coconut flakes or shreds and creamed coconut in sweet and savory dishes. Creamed coconut can be purchased online or at Asian grocery stores (see Resources, page 208).

tofu soy cream

MAKES 2 CUPS (500G)

12 ounces (340g) silken tofu

1/4 cup (60ml) unsweetened soy or almond milk (strained if homemade)

1/4 cup (60ml) pure maple syrup, plus more to taste

1 tablespoon freshly squeezed orange juice

1 1/2 teaspoons alcohol-free vanilla extract

Pinch of finely grated lemon zest

Throw all of the ingredients into your blender and blast on high for about 1 minute, until smooth and creamy. You may need to stop the machine and scrape down the sides of the container to get the creamiest results. If you want a sweeter cream, add more maple syrup to taste. Transfer to a bowl and chill in the fridge for a few hours to let the cream thicken slightly. It will keep in an airtight container in the fridge for up to 5 days.

variation: To make lemon soy cream, increase the orange juice to 2 tablespoons and the lemon zest to 1/4 teaspoon.

alkaline sugar-free cream

MAKES 1 CUP (225G)

1/2 cup (120ml) unsweetened almond milk (strained if homemade)

1/2 cup (90g) firmly packed young Thai coconut meat (see note, page 200)

1/4 cup (35g) blanched slivered raw almonds, soaked (see page 22)

1 teaspoon alcohol-free vanilla extract, plus more to taste

20 drops Sweet Leaf Vanilla Crème alcohol-free liquid stevia (see page 39)

10 drops Sweet Leaf English Toffee alcohol-free liquid stevia

Throw all of the ingredients into your blender and blast on high for 1 to 2 minutes, until smooth and creamy. You may need to stop the machine and scrape down the sides of the container to get the creamiest results. Tweak the vanilla to taste. Transfer to a bowl and chill in the fridge for at least 3 hours. This cream tastes even better the next day, and will keep in an airtight container in the fridge for up to 3 days.

This alkaline spread is almost too good to be true; it is full of healthy fats and oils and tastes delicious. It acts just like conventional butter: it's hard when it's cold, it's soft at room temperature, and it melts when spread on hot toast, breads, or muffins. I love to add the optional garlic and turmeric, which makes the blend more complex and tones down the coconut flavor. Note that the sweet variation is not alkaline. Either version will keep in the fridge for up to 1 month, but it never lasts that long.

healthy butter?

MAKES 1 CUP (250G)

½ cup (120ml) coconut oil in liquid form

¼ cup (60ml) cold-pressed extra-virgin olive oil

1 cup (140g) blanched raw almonds, raw macadamias, or raw unsalted cashews (unsoaked)

1½ teaspoons garlic powder, plus more to taste (optional)

¼ teaspoon natural salt (see box, page 38)

Pinch of ground turmeric (optional)

Throw all of the ingredients into your blender and blast on high for 1 to 2 minutes, until smooth and creamy. You may need to stop the machine and scrape down the sides of the container to get the creamiest results. Transfer the butter (which will be in liquid form) into a jar and chill in the fridge overnight to harden.

variation: To make sweet maple butter, replace the ¼ cup (60ml) of olive oil with additional coconut oil, omit the garlic powder and turmeric, and add 2 tablespoons pure maple syrup, plus more to taste.

This multi-purpose sauce tastes like commercial varieties, but skips the additives, preservatives, and sugar. It's also a great way to hoodwink the kids (and some adults) into eating their vegetables. I've deliberately scaled this recipe to a generous yield. The sauce freezes well, and can be used for last-minute pasta dishes, pizzas, lasagna, and vegetables. Don't cut down the quantities to make a smaller batch or you'll be sorry when you run out. You can also enjoy this sauce unblended. (Wait . . . did I just say that?)

sneaky veggie pasta and pizza sauce

MAKES 10 CUPS (2.5L)

1 tablespoon olive oil or grapeseed oil

4 cloves garlic, chopped

1 red onion, roughly chopped

Natural salt (see box, page 38) and freshly ground black pepper

2 ribs celery, diced

1 carrot, grated

1 zucchini, grated

1 long yellow squash, chopped

1 large red bell pepper, seeded and diced

10 medium-ripe tomatoes, roughly chopped

2 (14.5-ounce/411g) cans diced tomatoes

2 tablespoons tomato paste

1 tablespoon chopped fresh or 1 teaspoon dried oregano

1 tablespoon chopped fresh or 1 teaspoon dried thyme

1/2 cup (25g) chopped flat-leaf parsley

1/4 cup (6g) chopped basil

1 1/2 cups (360ml) vegetable broth (see page 115)

Heat the oil in a large saucepan over medium heat. Add the garlic, onion, 1/4 teaspoon of salt and 1/8 teaspoon of pepper and saute for about 5 minutes, until the onion is soft and translucent. Add the celery, carrot, zucchini, squash, and bell pepper and sauté for 5 minutes more, stirring occasionally. Stir in the fresh tomatoes, the canned tomatoes and their juice, the tomato paste, and the herbs. Add the vegetable broth, increase the heat to high, and bring just to a boil. Reduce the heat to medium and simmer, uncovered, for 15 minutes. Season with 1/4 teaspoon of salt and 1/8 teaspoon of pepper and simmer for 15 minutes more. Remove the saucepan from the heat and allow the sauce to cool slightly. Pour the sauce into your blender in batches and puree on high for 1 to 2 minutes, until creamy. (Remember to remove the plastic cap in the blender top and cover the opening with a kitchen towel so steam can escape while you blend.) Season with salt and pepper to taste. Store this in an airtight container in the fridge for up to 1 week, or in the freezer for up to 3 months.

You can tweak this all-purpose chocolate sauce to your preference. Add some spices or cayenne for a delicious kick. Use fewer cashews for a thinner sauce, or more cashews for a thick, fudge-like consistency. This sauce sets like a firm pudding when chilled, so topped with berries and cream, it serves up well as a rich chocolate dessert. Chocoholics beware: this one's intensely addictive.

dark chocolate sauce

MAKES 1¹/₂ CUPS (360ML)

1 cup (240ml) unsweetened almond milk (strained if homemade)

¹/₂ cup (35g) cacao powder or unsweetened cocoa powder, plus more to taste

¹/₂ cup (70g) raw unsalted cashews, soaked (see page 22), plus more to taste

¹/₄ cup (60ml) cold-pressed coconut oil in liquid form

¹/₄ cup (60ml) pure maple syrup or raw agave nectar, plus more to taste

1 teaspoon alcohol-free vanilla extract

Pinch of natural salt (optional; see page 38)

Throw all of the ingredients into your blender and mix on low for a few seconds so the cacao doesn't explode onto the sides and lid. Ramp up the speed to high and blend for 1 to 2 minutes, until smooth and creamy. Tweak flavors to taste (you may want more cacao or sweetener), and blend to your desired consistency (add more cashews if you want a thicker sauce).

This sauce is best used as soon as it's made. It will keep in the fridge for up to 3 days, but it naturally solidifies. In that case, let it stand at room temperature for about an hour, or heat it gently on the stove before using.

You may never cook or buy cranberry sauce again after you whip up this tasty raw version. You can make it in five minutes, and the chia seeds thicken the sauce like magic in just a half hour. Filled with live enzymes and vibrant fresh flavors, this holiday staple rocks.

quick cranberries

MAKES 2½ CUPS (630G)

2 cups (240g) cranberries, fresh or defrosted frozen

1 orange, peeled and segmented

½ cup (120ml) freshly squeezed orange juice

¼ cup (60ml) pure maple syrup

1 teaspoon minced ginger, plus more to taste

1 teaspoon finely grated orange zest, plus more to taste

¼ teaspoon ground cinnamon, plus more to taste

2 tablespoons black or white chia seeds

Put the cranberries, orange, orange juice, maple syrup, ginger, zest, and cinnamon into your blender and puree on low to medium for 10 to 15 seconds, until well combined but still a bit chunky. (If you prefer smooth cranberry sauce, blend on high.) Add the chia seeds and blend on low for just a few seconds, until they're incorporated but not fully blended. Tweak flavors to taste (you may want more ginger, orange zest, or cinnamon). Transfer the sauce to a sealed container and chill in the fridge for about 30 minutes, until the sauce has thickened. This will keep in the fridge for up to 5 days.

You don't have to coat-check your colon to indulge in this creamy béchamel sauce. Cauliflower is one of my top ten desert-island foods, and boy does it deliver in spectacular fashion here. Use this simple sauce as a topping for vegan lasagna, or add some miso or vegan cheese for a delicious, creamy sauce for pasta or vegetables. When serving this with pasta, you'll want to crank up the garlic, onion, and nutmeg and stir in some fresh herbs like parsley, rosemary, and thyme. This one's a winner, and it doesn't stick to your thighs.

béchamel sauce

MAKES 2³/₄ CUPS (650ML)

1 head cauliflower, cut into florets (about 4 cups/480g)

1¹/₂ tablespoons olive oil

1 teaspoon finely chopped garlic (about 1 clove)

1 yellow onion, diced

³/₄ teaspoon natural salt (see box, page 38), plus more to taste

³/₄ cup (180ml) unsweetened soy or almond milk (strained if homemade)

Pinch of ground nutmeg, plus more to taste

¹/₈ teaspoon freshly ground white pepper, plus more to taste

Place the cauliflower into a pot fitted with a steamer. Add just enough water to reach the bottom of the steamer, set the pot over high heat, and cover. Steam the cauliflower for 10 to 15 minutes, until tender. Remove the cauliflower and set aside.

Heat the oil in a saucepan over medium heat. Add the garlic, onion, and ¹/₄ teaspoon of the salt and sauté for 10 to 15 minutes, until the onion just begins to turn golden. Place the steamed cauliflower and the onion mixture into your blender, add the milk, and puree on high for 30 to 60 seconds, until smooth and creamy. Transfer the mixture to a saucepan over low heat. Add the nutmeg, the remaining ¹/₂ teaspoon of salt, and the pepper and warm for 5 minutes to let the flavors fuse. Tweak flavors to taste (you may want a bit more salt, nutmeg, or pepper). This will keep in an airtight container in the fridge for up to 5 days.

To reheat, warm the sauce in a small saucepan over low to medium heat, stirring occasionally, for 2 to 3 minutes, until heated through.

Served over tofu or tempeh, potatoes, and other vegetables, this blender take on a classic gravy is simple and delicious. I love the delicate flavor of thyme, but you could add any herbs and spices that tickle your fancy. Make this gravy your own.

classic white gravy

MAKES 1 TO 1¹/₂ CUPS (240 TO 360ML)

1 tablespoon olive oil or grapeseed oil

2 cups (300g) diced yellow onion

Natural salt (see box, page 38)

1 teaspoon minced garlic (about 1 clove)

1¹/₂ cups (360ml) vegetable broth (see page 115)

3¹/₂ ounces (100g) firm tofu

2 teaspoons white miso paste

¹/₂ teaspoon chopped thyme

Freshly ground white pepper

1 tablespoon kuzu-root starch (see Resources, page 208) or cornstarch plus 1 tablespoon water, as needed to thicken (optional)

Heat the oil in a saucepan over medium heat. Add the onions and a pinch of salt and sauté for about 5 minutes, until the onions are soft and translucent. Add the garlic and sauté for 2 minutes more. Put the onion and garlic mixture into your blender and add ¹/₂ cup (120ml) of the broth, the tofu, miso, thyme, and a pinch of white pepper and blend on high for 30 to 60 seconds, until smooth and creamy. Return the blend to the saucepan over medium heat and stir for 2 minutes. Whisk in the remaining 1 cup (240ml) of broth and bring to a boil. Reduce the heat to medium and simmer for about 10 minutes, until the gravy reduces and coats a spoon thickly. If you prefer a thicker consistency, combine the starch and water in a small bowl to make a paste. Add the paste to the saucepan and simmer for 10 minutes more. Season with white pepper to taste. The gravy will keep stored in an airtight container in the fridge for up to 1 week. To reheat, warm it in a saucepan over low heat.

resources: get your goods here

alkaline supplies and resources

AlkaViva
alkaviva.com
Alkaline water machines.

iHerb
iherb.com
World Organic or NOW Foods liquid chlorophyll.

Miracle Clay
miracleclay.net/magento
Edible clay and body products.

Nikken PiMag Waterfall
nikken.com
Water-filtration systems.

pH Ion Balance
phionbalance.com
Test strips.

pH Miracle Living
phmiracleliving.com
Mineral salts and lifestyle products.

Santevia
santevia.com
Alkaline jugs and bottles.

Vitacost
vitacost.com
World Organic liquid chlorophyll.

appliances

Breville
brevilleusa.com
Blenders and other appliances.

Excalibur
excaliburdehydrator.com
Dehydrators.

KitchenAid
kitchenaid.com
Blenders and other appliances.

Nutribullet
nutribullet.com
Blenders.

Omega
omegajuicers.com
Blenders and juicers.

Oster
oster.com
Blenders.

Vitamix
vitamix.com
Blenders.

coconut products

Coconut Secret
coconutsecret.com
Nectar, aminos, flour, and sweeteners.

Edward & Sons
edwardandsons.com
Let's Do . . . Organic dried and creamed coconut.

Exotic Superfoods
exoticsuperfoods.com
Raw coconut meat and water.

Nutiva
nutiva.com
Oil.

Tropical Traditions
tropicaltraditons.com
Various products.

cold-pressed oils

Omega Nutrition
omeganutrition.com

Spectrum Organics
spectrumorganics.com

cultured (probiotic-rich) supplies

Body Ecology
bodyecology.com
Starters, foods, and supplements.

Cultures For Health
culturesforhealth.com
Starters, kefir, kombucha, and fermentation supplies.

iHerb
iherb.com
Solaray and Jarrow Formulas probiotic supplements.

VSL#3
shop.vsl3.com
Probiotic supplements.

cultured (probiotic-rich) food and drinks

Farmhouse Culture
farmhouseculture.com
Cultured vegetables.

GT's Kombucha
synergydrinks.com
Kombucha.

Healing Movement
healingmovement.net
Cultured vegetables and coconut water kefir.

Kevita
kevita.com
Probiotic drinks.

Tonix Botanical Solutions
mytonix.com
Coconut water kefir.

gluten-free grains and vegan pasta

Ancient Harvest Quinoa
quinoa.net
Quinoa and quinoa pasta.

Arrowhead Mills
arrowheadmills.com
Various products.

Lundberg
lundberg.com
Brown rice and brown-rice pasta.

Tinkyada
tinkyada.com
Brown-rice pasta.

hemp products

Manitoba Harvest
manitobaharvest.com
Various products.

herbs, spices, flavorings, and seasonings

Amazon
amazon.com
Cortas rose water and orange blossom water.

Bragg
bragg.com
Liquid aminos and apple cider vinegar.

Cold Mountain Miso
coldmountainmiso.com
Miso.

Eden Foods
edenfoods.com
Gomasio.

Frontier Natural Products
frontiercoop.com
Alcohol-free flavors and extracts.

Herbamare and Trocomare
herbamare.us
Proprietary herb and salt blends.

Miso Master
great-eastern-sun.com
Organic miso pastes.

Mountain Rose Herbs
mountainroseherbs.com
Herbs, spices, and essential oils.

San-J
san-j.com
Wheat-free tamari.

The Spice Hunter
spicehunter.com
Various spices.

Spicely Organic Spices
spicely.com
Various spices.

kitchenware

Amazon
amazon.com
Various products.

Dreamfarm
dreamfarm.com
Kitchen tools.

Eco Jarz
ecojarz.com
Jars, lids, and stainless-steel straws.

Glass Dharma
glassdharma.com
Glass straws.

Le Creuset
lecreuset.com
Cookware and tools.

Oxo
oxo.com
Ice cube trays.

Sur La Table
surlatable.com
Various products.

Tovolo
tovolo.com
Silicone ice-cube molds.

Williams-Sonoma
williams-sonoma.com
Various products.

Casa
casa.com
World Cuisine vegetable spiral slicer.

milks

Flax USA
flaxusa.com
Flax milk.

Living Harvest
livingharvest.com
Hemp milk.

One Lucky Duck
oneluckyduck.com
Nut milk bags.

Pacific Natural Foods
pacificfoods.com
Variety of plant-based milks.

Rice Dream
tastethedream.com
Rice milk.

Lekithos Inc.
mysunflowerlecithin.com
Sunflower seed lecithin.

natural sweeteners

Amazon
amazon.com
Plantation unsulphured blackstrap molasses.

Coconut Secret
coconutsecret.com
Coconut crystals and coconut nectar.

Maple Valley
maplevalleysyrup.coop
Organic maple syrup and maple sugar.

Navitas Naturals
navitas.com
Coconut sugar, yacon syrup, and lucuma powder.

Nu Naturals
nunaturals.com
Alcohol-free stevia.

Organic Nectars
organicnectars.com
Raw agave nectar.

SweetLeaf
sweetleaf.com
Alcohol-free and flavored stevia.

Wholesome Sweeteners
wholesomesweeteners.com
Various natural sweeteners.

raw nuts and seeds

Raw Nuts and Seeds
rawnutsandseeds.com
Various products.

Sun Butter
sunbutter.com
Nut-free sunflower seed butter.

Vivapura
vivapura.com
Best nut butters ever!

organic fresh produce

Driscoll's
driscolls.com
Organic berries.

Earthbound Farm
ebfarm.com
Fruits and vegetables.

Kenter Canyon Farms
kentercanyonfarms.com
Lettuces and herbs.

Melissa's Produce
melissas.com
Fruits and vegetables.

Organic Girl
iloveorganicgirl.com
Leafy greens.

protein and green powders

Garden of Life
gardenoflife.com
Raw powders.

Growing Naturals
growingnaturals.com
Rice and pea powders.

Manitoba Harvest
manitobaharvest.com
Hemp powders.

Sprout Living
sproutliving.com
Raw and sprouted powders.

Sun Warrior
sunwarrior.com
Protein and ormus supergreens.

Vega
myvega.com
Great plant-based blends.

salt

Celtic Sea Salt
celticseasalt.com

Himala Salt
himalasalt.com

Real Salt
realsalt.com

sea vegetables

Eden Foods
edenfoods.com

Ironbound Island Seaweed
ironboundisland.com

Maine Coast
seaveg.com

specialty foods

Earth Circle Organics
earthcircleorganics.com
Raw foods.

iHerb
iherb.com
Natural ingredients and supplements.

Neera's Cinnabar Specialty Foods
cinnabar.com
Tamarind paste, chutney, and sauces.

starches/ thickeners

Eden Foods
edenfoods.com
Kuzu-root powder.

Edward & Sons
edwardandsons.com
Let's Do . . . Organic cornstarch and tapioca starch.

superfoods

Navitas Naturals
navitasnaturals.com
Various products.

vegan ingredients

Annie's Naturals
www.annies.com
Worcestershire sauce.

Daiya
daiyafoods.com
Cheese.

Dandies
chicagoveganfoods.com
Marshmallows.

Edward & Sons
edwardandsons.com
The Wizard's gluten-free Worcestershire sauce.

Enjoy Life
enjoylifefoods.com
Chocolate chips.

Follow Your Heart
followyourheart.com
Mayonnaise.

Kite Hill
kite-hill.com
Cheese.

vegetable broth

Massel
massel.com
Bouillon cubes.

great reading

alkalinity

The Acid-Alkaline Food Guide: A Quick Reference to Foods & Their Effect on pH Levels by Susan E. Brown and Larry Trivieri, Jr. (Square One Pub, Second Edition, 2013).

Alkalize or Die: Superior Health Through Proper Alkaline-Acid Balance by Theodore A. Baroody (Holographic Health Inc., 1991).

The pH Miracle: Balance Your Diet, Reclaim Your Health by Dr. Robert O. Young and Shelley Redford Young (Grand Central Life & Style, Revised Edition, 2010).

Water & Salt: The Essence of Life by Barbara Hendel and Peter Ferreira (Natural Resources, 2003).

food combining

Fit for Life by Harvey and Marilyn Diamond (Grand Central Life & Style, 2010).

Food Combining for Health: Get Fit with Foods that Don't Fight by Doris Grant and Jean Joice (Healing Arts Press, 1985).

Food Combining Made Easy by Herbert M. Shelton (Book Pub Company, Third Edition, 2012).

Proper Food Combining Works: Living Testimony by Lee Dubelle (Nutri Books Corp., 1987).

The Raw Energy Bible by Leslie Kenton (Vermilion, 2001).

general health and food politics

Ayurveda: The Science of Self-Healing by Dr. Vasant Lad (Lotus Press, 1985).

The Botany of Desire: A Plant's-Eye View of the World by Michael Pollan (Random House, 2002).

The China Study: The Most Comprehensive Study of Nutrition Ever Conducted and the Startling Implications for Diet, Weight Loss, and Long-Term Health by T. Collin Campbell and Thomas M. Campbell II (BenBella Books, 2006).

Clean: The Revolutionary Program to Restore the Body's Natural Ability to Heal Itself by Alejandro Junger, MD (HarperOne, Second Updated Edition, 2012).

Clean Gut: The Breakthrough Plan for Eliminating the Root Cause of Disease and Revolutionizing Your Health by Alejandro Junger, MD (HarperOne, 2013).

The Coconut Oil Miracle by Bruce Fife and Jon J. Kabara (Avery Trade, Fifth Edition, 2013).

The Colon Health Handbook: New Health Through Colon Rejuvenation by Robert Gray (Emerald Pub, Twelfth Revised Edition, 1990).

Cooked: A Natural History of Transformation by Michael Pollan (Penguin Press, 2013).

Diet for a New America by John Robbins (HJ Kramer/New World Library, 25th Anniversary Edition, 2012).

Eat for Health by Joel Fuhrman (Gift of Health Press, Revised Single Paperback Edition, 2012).

Eat Right 4 Your Type: The Individualized Diet Solution to Staying Healthy, Living Longer & Achieving Your Ideal Weight by Dr. Peter J. D'Adamo (Putnam Adult, 1997).

Flax the Super Food!: Over 80 Delicious Recipes Using Flax Oil and Ground Flaxseed by Barb Bloomfield, Judy Brown, and Siegfried Gursche (Book Publishing Company, 2000).

Food Matters: A Guide to Conscious Eating by Mark Bittman (Simon & Schuster, 2009).

The Food Revolution: How Your Diet Can Help Save Your Life and Our World by John Robbins (Conari Press, Tenth Revised Edition, 2010).

Food Rules: An Eater's Manual by Michael Pollan (Penguin Books, 2009).

Grain Brain: The Surprising Truth about Wheat, Carbs, and Sugar—Your Brain's Silent Killers by David Perlmutter, MD (Little, Brown and Company, 2013).

Healing with Whole Foods: Asian Traditions and Modern Nutrition by Paul Pitchford (North Atlantic Books, Third Revised Expanded Edition, 2002).

In Defense of Food: An Eater's Manifesto by Michael Pollan (Penguin Books, 2009).

Know Your Fats: The Complete Primer for Understanding the Nutrition of Fats, Oils, and Cholesterol by Mary G. Enig (Bethesda Press, 2010).

The Macrobiotic Way by Michio Kushi, Stephen Blauer, and Wendy Esko (Avery Trade, Third Edition, 2004).

Nourishing Traditions: The Cookbook that Challenges Politically Correct Nutrition and the Diet Dictocrats by Sally Fallon (Newtrends Publishing Inc., Revised and Updated Second Edition, 2003).

Nutrition and Physical Degeneration by Weston A. Price (Price Pottenger Nutrition, Eighth Edition, 2008).

The Omega Diet: The Lifesaving Nutritional Program Based on the Diet of the Island of Crete by Artemis P. Simopoulos and Jo Robinson (Harper, 1999).

The Omnivore's Dilemma: A Natural History of Four Meals by Michael Pollan (Penguin, 2007).

Salt Sugar Fat: How the Food Giants Hooked Us by Michael Moss (Random House, 2013).

Silent Spring by Rachel Carson (Houghton Mifflin Company, Anniversary Edition, 2002).

Superfoods: The Food and Medicine of the Future by David Wolfe (North Atlantic Books, 2009).

The Tao of Health, Sex & Longevity: A Modern Practical Guide to the Ancient Way by Daniel P. Reid (Fireside, 1989).

Thrive: The Vegan Nutrition Guide to Optimal Performance in Sports and Life by Brendan Brazier (Da Capo Lifelong Books, 2008).

Wheat Belly: Lose the Wheat, Lose the Weight, and Find Your Path Back to Health by William Davis, MD (Rodale Books, 2011).

probiotics for health

The Body Ecology Diet: Recovering Your Health and Rebuilding Your Immunity by Donna Gates (Hay House, Revised Edition, 2011).

The Candida Cure: Yeast, Fungus & Your Health by Ann Boroch (Quintessential Healing Inc, Revised Edition, 2009).

Wild Fermentation: The Flavor, Nutrition, and Craft of Live-Culture Foods by Sandor Ellix Katz (Chelsea Green Publishing, 2003).

The Yeast Connection: A Medical Breakthrough by William G. Crook, MD (Square One Publishers, 2007).

raw foods

Conscious Eating by Gabriel Cousens, MD (North Atlantic Books, Second Edition, 2000).

Eating for Beauty by David Wolfe (North Atlantic Books, 2003).

Enzyme Nutrition by Dr. Edward Howell (Avery Publishing Group, 1995).

Food Enzymes for Health & Longevity by Dr. Edward Howell (Lotus Press, Second Edition, 1994).

Green for Life: The Updated Classic on Green Smoothie Nutrition by Victoria Boutenko (North Atlantic Books, 2010).

The Hippocrates Diet and Health Program by Anne Wigmore (Avery Trade, 1983).

The Sunfood Diet Success System by David Wolfe (North Atlantic Books, Seventh Edition, 2008).

websites

Dr. Annemarie Colbin, foodandhealing.com

Dr. Joel Fuhrman, drfuhrman.com

Gerson Institute, gerson.org

Hippocrates Health Institute, hippocratesinst.org

Dr. Mark Hyman, drhyman.com

Kushi Institute, kushiinstitute.org

Dr. Joseph Mercola, mercola.com

Dr. Mehmet Oz, doctoroz.com

Michael Pollan, michaelpollan.com

Raw Family, rawfamily.com

Tree of Life, treeoflife.nu

Dr. Andrew Weil, drweil.com

Weston A. Price Foundation, westonaprice.org

David Wolfe, davidwolfe.com

The World's Healthiest Foods, whfoods.com

acknowledgments

If it takes a village to raise a child, it stands to reason that it takes an amazing publisher, a brilliant editor, a team of awesome agents, a tenacious publicist, a savvy attorney, a genius photographer, a master food stylist, over fifty committed recipe testers, generous and loving friends, and the most incredible family and partner in the world to birth a blender cookbook.

I was supported every step of the way by this cast of sensational characters, and my gratitude is overflowing. These remarkable folks are the very best at what they do, and in some instances, that simply means just loving me.

The Dream Team: Sharon Bowers, Alex Kakoyiannis, Jess Taylor, and Joe Stallone. Thanks for breathing deeply with me at every turn! Your talent, honesty, humor, and unwavering belief instilled me with just the right amount of confidence.

The Perfect Storm: An incomparable force at Ten Speed Press, including Aaron Wehner, Hannah Rahill, Julie Bennett, Emma Campion, Kelly Snowden, Michele Crim, Betsy Stromberg, Kristin Casemore, Ali Slagle, Erin Welke, and Daniel Wikey. I'm humbled by your gentle but savvy, always collaborative way of guiding this project, and your respect for my aesthetic sensibility. A dream experience for a first-time author. A special nod to Kelly, who initiated my love affair with this great publishing house. Immeasurable thanks to the incredible David Drake, Carisa Hays, Kimberly Snead, Jill Greto, Candice Chaplin, Pam Roman, Daryl Mattson, Liisa McCloy-Kelley, and the rest of the crew at the Crown Publishing Group and Random House for your incredible support.

Thank you to the ludicrously talented Anson Smart, David Morgan, Olivia Andrews, Russell Horton, Samantha Powell, Inez Garcia, Josefine Brodd, Sunny Kang, Jerrie-Joy Redman-Lloyd, Tilly Pamment, Roxie Smart, and Maria Esztergalyos for bringing my vision to vivid life in spectacular fashion. Special thanks to Jody Scott, for bringing us all together, and to my dear friend Susan Stitt, for shooting the behind-the-scenes video footage, and for unflagging support during the shoot.

For generously providing items to help with the production and photography, I want to thank some of my favorite brands: Williams-Sonoma, West Elm, Anthropologie, Vitamix, Breville, KitchenAid, Omega, Oster, NutriBullet, Excalibur, Le Creuset, Dreamfarm, GLOBAL knives, Cutco, Ruhlin Group, Eco Jarz, Navitas Naturals, SweetLeaf, Maxwell & Williams, Dinosaur Designs, Koskela, MUD Australia, Di Lorenzo Tiles, Cloth Fabric, The Forty-nine Studio, Onsite Supply & Design, HUB, Laura Mercier, Lee Mathews, and Melissa's Produce. And special thanks to Georgie Sulzberger and Merrick Watts for allowing us to use your exquisite home.

Publishing offers don't just fall from the sky. Huge thanks goes to Dean White, Kelly Bock, and Olivia MacKenzie-Smith for developing my brand in the early stages, and to Kane McErvale and Jenelle Rayson from Verve Portraits for the photographic magic. To Gina Smith, who keeps my life running smoothly, and to my genius web designer, Maxwell Hibbert, who makes everything I do look sensational.

This book could be titled "90 Recipes Tested in 90 Days." With Scott recording in our home studio, directly below the kitchen, I needed a venue for off-site testing. My friends rallied, in stupendous generosity, opening up their kitchens and lives.

A special thanks to the unstoppable Denise Chamberlain, the ultimate blending champion. What fun we had! I don't know what I would have done without you. To my soul sister, Stacey Aswad, for sharing your brilliant cooking skills, keen taste buds, and love; and to Chuck Duran, for dipping your humorous spoon into the mix. To the inspiring Geoffrey Rodriguez and Bernhard Punzet, both shining lights, and to G, for stupendous creativity in the kitchen. To the wonderful Michelle Smith-Aiken, Nikki Hansen, Eda Benjakul, Liz Von Schlegell, Flynn Tierney, Rei and Kai Chavez, George, Sue Jim, Toshiko, Selina, and Sean Mohr for cooking and laughing with me.

I was fortunate to have over fifty volunteer recipe testers, blending all over the world. Their constructive feedback was invaluable in the development of these recipes. I bow to my blending tribe: Amy and Dan Rubinate; Andrea Libretti, Jaclyn and Jade DiDonato, and Ed Halvorsen; Andrea Passarella; Anna Hanson; Charles Constant; Christine, Brad, Melia, and Jake Barlow; Darla and Robert Morello; Dawn Agran; Debbie, Chuck, and Christopher Pine; Jacque and Nathan Godwin; Alicia Elliot; Pola, Dave, and Mark Snell; Donna Richards and Tora Cullip; Duanne Hibbert; Elaine and Kathleen Morales, and Emily Bramhall; Elayne Jaye; Hillary Huber Wilson; Holly, Jason, and Zoey Ojalvo; Jennifer, Scott, Catherine, and Benjamin Ward; Judith Lewis; Karen Kipp and Bobby Herman; Kate Lewis and Devin Echle; Kathleen Podhajski-Brown and Taylor, Ella, Kendra, Hayden, and Gerard Brown; Kibby and Scott Miller; Kim, Simon, Cameron, Ripley, and Ziggy Tornya; Lisbeth Kennelly; Lori Robin Wilson; Magali, Alessia, and Andreas Pès Schmid; Marie-Guy Maynard, and Louis, Tomas, Jacob, and Lucas Subirana; Dr. Michelle Robin, Crystal Jenkins, Russ Swift, and Dr. Paul Jernigan; Nicki Whitfield and the students at Burwood Heights Primary School; Rachel and Joe Fulginiti; Robin and Jay Eller; Robyn Booth, and Paul, Thomas, Spencer, and Elliot Greenow; Sharon Geake and Scott Henderson; Sharon Huffman and Dr. Elaine Carter; Shez, Dean, Rocco, and Duke Cantlie; Stephen Rowan and Catherine Knowles; Tina, David, Andrew, and Matthew Allen; Vibeke Vale and Karen Kelly;

Dawnette Brady; and Wendi, Scott, Ava, and Danny Higginbotham.

Thank you to my performance agents: the crews at KMR Talent, AVO Talent, JE Talent, and EM Voices, and to Melissa Rose and Annette Robinson, for support, patience, and enthusiasm as I turned away other work to pursue this opportunity.

And to my loyal online readers and followers: your enthusiasm, steady engagement, and illuminating emails make a blogger's day every day.

A whole lot of love held me up through this journey. Thanks to Bill, Margot, Margot-Anne, and Kimberly Brick; and to John and Sandra Hanes, Mike Schmandt, and Debra Sharkey. To my little sister, Katy Townsend: thanks for the boundless love and workouts that kept me sane; and to the incomparable Mikaho Hara, the greatest kindred-spirit friend of my life.

To my unbelievable mum and dad, for unfailing love and support, and for supplying me the sharpest tools and best ingredients for blending up a happy and fulfilling life. You make everything sweeter. My divine sister, Kara Masters, thank you for toiling away in the kitchen, well out of your comfort zone, for an ever-ready healthy perspective, and for being my constant confidante. To my brother-in-law, Leigh Cassidy, for your discerning buds, and my darling niece and nephew, Alexandra and Sullivan, for your gorgeous Skype cheer dances, and for just being awesome little people.

To Cookie, for greeting me every day with a lick and a "you can do it" wag of that stumpy tail.

Finally, to my best friend and the love of my life, Scott, for showing up every day, nourishing me body and soul, holding my fears, and enriching my life with great stories.

index

All rights reserved.
Published in the United States by Ten Speed Press, an imprint of the Crown Publishing Group, a division of Random House LLC, a Penguin Random House Company, New York.
www.crownpublishing.com
www.tenspeed.com

Ten Speed Press and the Ten Speed Press colophon are registered trademarks of Random House LLC

Library of Congress Cataloging-in-Publication Data is on file with the publisher.

Trade Paperback ISBN:
978-1-60774-643-0
eBook ISBN: 978-1-60774-644-7

Printed in China

Design by Betsy Stromberg

10 9 8 7 6

First Edition